140 OVERLOAD GAMES AND FINISHING PRACTICES

by Michael Beale

REEDSWAIN PUBLISHING

**Library of Congress
Cataloging - in - Publication Data**

The Soccer Academy
140 Overload Games and Finishing Practices
by Michael Beale

ISBN-13: 978-1-59164-108-7
ISBN-10: 1-59164-108-X
Library of Congress Control Number: 2007926771
© 2007

Art Direction, Layout and Proofing
Bryan R. Beaver

Cover Photograph
© iStockphoto.com/Bruce Lonngren

Diagrams made with
easySportsGraphics
www.sports-graphics.com

Printed by
Data Reproductions
Auburn, Michigan

Reedswain Publishing
562 Ridge Road
Spring City, PA 19475
www. reedswain.com
info@reedswain.com

CONTENTS

Acknowledgements **v**

Introduction **vi**

Overload practices and small sided games **1**

Finishing practices **57**

Conclusion **149**

"The level of a coach can be noticed by the manner in which he inspires the players. That cannot be learned on a coaching course. It is the individual quality of each coach, the personality of the coach."

Rinus Michels
Legendary Dutch coach and the creator of Total Football

Acknowledgements

The writing of this book is dedicated in the memory of my two grandfathers, Bill and Fred and to my family for their love and support that gives me the belief and confidence in my work. I would also like to thank all the academy staff at Chelsea Football Club.

Introduction

I have been very fortunate that as a young coach I have had wonderful opportunities to be around professional football clubs for a number of years and had a chance to learn from experienced players and coaches.

From the age of two, a close family friend and ex Crystal Palace and Portsmouth player Billy Gilbert used to take me to watch him play and experience professional football on a regular basis. The late Raymond Harford, the former Luton and Wimbledon manager and most famously assistant to Kenny Dalglish at Blackburn Rovers was a relative. Just knowing these two men gave me the inner belief and confidence that it was possible to live the dream as both a professional football player and coach.

After spending eight years in the junior, youth and senior teams at Charlton Athletic and now 6 years as a full time coach, I have had the pleasure to play alongside some wonderful players and been coached and worked alongside some excellent coaches.

I have built my current beliefs through studying hard, listening and taking on board the experiences I have had so far. The sessions in this book are from my personal library of sessions that I have created in the past year. In creating each of the sessions I have tried to transfer my thoughts to that of a young player and in order to improve my players learning, enjoyment and ability, I always make sure the following statements are true

- The session is fun
- The players have freedom to express their individual ability
- The players have choices in movement and technique
- The players have to think and solve problems
- The session is realistic, challenging and competitive.

OVERLOAD PRACTICES AND SMALL SIDED GAMES

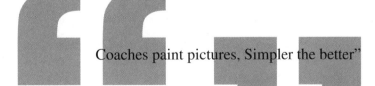

Coaches paint pictures, Simpler the better"

Overload practices and small sided games

I have studied many youth matches from u7 right up to u18 level, paying particular close attention to various attacking situations and taking pictures in my mind of the positioning of the players and the final outcomes. I then decided to create realistic and flowing sessions that have real game scenarios, positioning of players and starting points. The aim of the sessions is to improve our decision making, reactions, creativity and the understanding of various roles and playing positions.

The practices are designed to inspire and motivate the players in real game situations that give them freedom of choice and movement both in and out of possession. The basic techniques of passing, dribbling, shooting, tackling and heading will all be used but with use to solve a match problem rather than constant repetition. The sessions have goals and objectives for both the attacking and defending players in order to aid the tempo, competition and enjoyment of the practice.

The coach is only needed to establish the initial set up of the session and to ask the players questions on their choices and actions. The sessions all have little hints and cues that set the players down a certain learning path and enable the coach to see what he wants without necessarily instructing the players to do so.

The majority of the sessions include an overload [2v1, 3v2 etc] or at least an overload to start with. Matches are full of overloads both in attack and defence and therefore I base a big focus of my training time to overloads as they ultimately determine the final result of matches and success of teams.

The practices are listed starting with simple 2v1's and then increasing in number of players used and difficulty. The dimensions of the field should be judged by the individual coach by looking at the age and ability of players being coached and even though the sessions are aimed at improving attacking play, you can almost turn the sessions on their head and work on defensive priorities within the same set ups.

OVERLOAD PRACTICES AND SMALL SIDED GAMES

SESSION	TITLE
1.	2v1 OVERLAP
2.	2v1 TARGET REACTION
3.	2v1 TARGET MAN
4.	2v1[+1] RETREATING
5.	2v1 FACING AWAY
6.	2v1 CHOICE
7.	POSSESSION SUPPORT
8.	WIDE PLAYERS ATTACKING CROSSES FROM THE OTHER WING
9.	3v2 BREAKTHROUGH DRIBBLE
10.	3v2 SWITCH PLAY
11.	3v2 VARIOUS ANGLES
12.	3v2 OVERLOAD
13.	4v3 SWITCH TO GAIN ADVANTAGE
14.	1v1 CONTINUOUS
15.	3v2 [+gk] CONTINUOUS
16.	4v2 [+2] HUNTING AS A TEAM
17.	2v2 EIGHT BALL GAME
18.	MULTI BALL GAME
19.	3v2 [+1] MIDFIELD RETREAT
20.	5v5 TRANSITION
21.	3 GAMES IN 1
22.	OVERLOAD GAMES
23.	4v2 BECOMES 2v1
24.	4v4 [+4] GAME
25.	3v1 [+2] OVERLOAD
26.	3v1 POSSESSION SUPPORT
27.	TEAM POSSESSION UNDER PRESSURE
28.	4 PLAYER TECHNIQUE CIRCUIT
29.	3v3 BECOMES 6v6
30.	TEAM 1v1 BATTLES
31.	3v3 MIDFIELD/DEFENCE PRESSURE AND SHAPE
32.	3v3 ATTACKERS PRESSING FROM THE FRONT
33.	3v1 TWO TEAM BATTLE
34.	2v2 DEFENDING PRINCIPLES
35.	4v3[+1] ATTACK AND DEFEND
36.	8v4 POSSESSION UNDER PRESSURE
37.	5v3 TWO GOALS REVERSE GAME
38.	4v4 ATTACK V DEFENCE
39.	6v6 BLOCKING THE PASSING GAPS
40.	3v2 COUNTER GAME
41.	3v3 COUNTER GAME WITH WIDE PLAYERS
42.	3v3 ATTACK AND DEFEND
43.	SWITCHING PLAY AND ATTACKING THE SPACE
44.	SWITCHING PLAY AND ATTACKING THE SPACE –PROGRESSION 1
45.	SWITCHING PLAY AND ATTACKING THE SPACE –PROGRESSION 2
46.	4v4 DEFENDING FROM THE FRONT
47.	3v3 DRIBBLING WITH THE BALL GAME
48.	3v2 OVERLAPPING IN THE FINAL THIRD
49.	3v2 WIDE PLAYER GETTING PAST HIS FORWARD
50.	3v2 OVERLAPPING IN THE FINAL 3RD
51.	3v2 QUICK COUNTER
52.	HUNTING TO WIN POSSESSION AND ATTACK

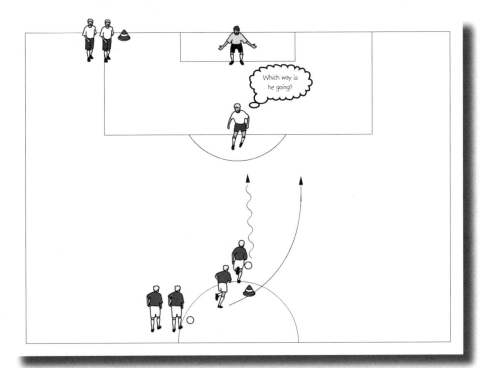

SET-UP

⊙ 2 groups of players. Defenders by the side of the goal and attackers that work in pairs. The first defender comes out to the middle of the pitch. One attacker starts 5 yards in front of the other with a ball at his feet.

⊙ To start the practice, the first attacker dribbles at the defender. The second attacker makes a run off the first attacker's shoulder to make an overlap. The 2v1 continues until a goal is scored or the ball leaves play.

THOUGHTS

The practice forces various choices and decisions to be made. The first attacker must be direct and then read where his teammate is overlapping. Should I pass? Or do I use my teammate's run as a decoy? The second attacker must communicate with his teammate to let him know which side he is going. Could the player make a dummy run one way and then quickly change direction to try to confuse the defender?

SET-UP

⊛ This session has two groups competing against each other with the coach acting as the initial server.

⊛ One player from each team goes to the middle of the pitch and gets into space to act as a forward. The coach then passes to either the team on his left or his right. Whichever midfielder receives the ball immediately dribbles in to make a 2v1 with his teammate. The other player must now react as a defender and try to stop them.

⊛ Once you have been a dribbling midfielder you then become a forward. If you have been a defender you must stay in the middle and wait to have your turn as a forward.

THOUGHTS

The practice works on movement and reactions of the first two attackers, how do they react to becoming a forward and how do they react to becoming the defender? What movements do they make to receive? The midfielder has to be direct in his dribbling and either combine with his teammate to score or use him as a decoy. The midfielder may also have the opportunity of making a quick pass to the forward as the defender may be slow in reacting; therefore the practice ensures quick and decisive play.

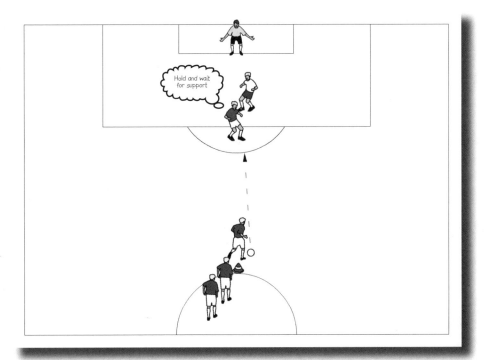

SET-UP

- 3 roles to play: midfielder, center forward and then central defender. After being a midfielder you then move up to play as a forward and then the defender before resting.

- To start the practice the forward makes a movement to lose his defender and then receives a pass from the midfielder, then a 2v1 game commences until a goal is scored, the keeper saves or the ball leaves play.

THOUGHTS
This is a simple practice that should be used with young players. The session forces the forward to make realistic movements to receive the ball and then show good hold-up play. The midfielder is forced to support the initial pass, look for a return and then the two attackers must show good combination play to finish.

SET-UP

- Three groups of players: two attacking groups, one to the left and one to the right and one defending group in the middle.

- The first defender goes out as a central defender and one of the attackers starts as a center forward.

- The middle players start with the ball and pass to the team on the right. Immediately the right attacker dribbles to make a 2v1, the defender must try to hold up play while the middle defender tries to recover as quickly as possible in order to stop the attackers combining to score.

- The middle defender becomes the central defender and the wide attacker becomes the center forward. The next practice starts with the ball going out to the left.

THOUGHTS

This practice ensures quick play from the attackers. The wide player must be direct in his play, also the forward must make a clever run and pull off his marker in order to receive a pass. The central defender has to try and hold-up play. Does he pressure the wide attacker? Or stay with the forward? How quickly can the middle defender recover and where does he recover to?

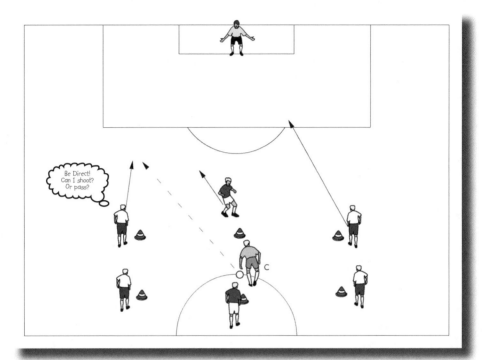

SET-UP

- Players work in groups of three, one player acts as a defender and goes in the middle. The player acting as a defender must face away from his goal to start.
- The coach starts the practice by playing a through ball to one of the attackers. The attacker not in possession must make a supporting run whilst the defender must turn and recover.
- The groups rotate and all have a turn as the defender.

THOUGHTS
Normally 2v1 defending and attacking situations are played with the attackers facing a defender, but often in a game the opposite happens and the ball is played into space behind the defender. This practice looks at the choices given to the attacker in possession: Does he decide to shoot or pass? Does he make the most of his situation by playing at speed or does he enable the defender to recover? The attacker not in possession must also make a decision: Does he attack the box in hope of a cross or rebounded shot? Or does he pull back in order to support from behind or receive a set back?

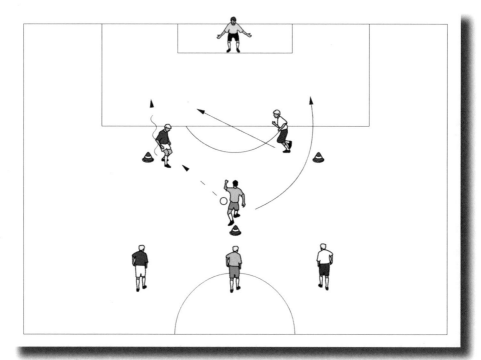

SET-UP

⊙ Groups of 3 players

⊙ One player starts ten yards behind the other two and starts the practice by playing a pass into one of the players. Immediately the other player acts as a defender and tries to stop the two players finishing.

⊙ The defender acts as the starting player in the next attack.

THOUGHTS

Young players tend to stand and watch after they have made a good pass or as a teammate is running to goal. This practice ensures a player supports his initial pass and either follows up and finishes from a rebounded shot or receives a return pass in an advanced position. The defender also has choices to make: Does he react well? Does he decide to force the player wide? Or does he decide to get goal side and hold him up?

SET-UP

- 3 groups of 4 players: 2 groups working, the other acting as target players as shown in the diagram.
- The players have to make five one-touch passes in the first area before transferring the ball to the next target player and then supporting to repeat in the next zone.
- The game lasts for 1-2 minutes with the team who completes the most sets being the winners.
- The teams rotate and all have a go at being the target players.

THOUGHTS

This session is good when looking at quick passing, movement and then finally support from the whole group. The competition against the other group ensures a good tempo and concentration from each player.

SET-UP

- 3 groups, left midfield, right midfielder and attacker/defender
- Starts off with the attacker's movement to receive. He receives a pass from the midfielder and plays out into space for either wide player.
- The wide player who receives the pass dribbles down the wing and crosses for both the attacker and other wide player who try to lose the defender and score.
- The attacker becomes the defender in the next attack
- Players rotate between being middle players and wide players.

THOUGHTS

Many young players switch off when the ball is not on their side of the pitch. A wide player who is clever and aware enough to always attack the far post on crosses from the other side can find himself in many goal scoring situations.

SET-UP

- Two groups of four players
- One group works in the attacking zone and plays 2v2, each taking turns to be the attackers and defenders. The other four players take two balls each and line up behind the cones/mannequins.
- The coach calls out the name of one of the outside players and that player dribbles at the flag, does a skill and goes past him to make a 3v2 situation with the two attacking players.
- The attackers and defenders rotate roles until all eight balls have been played. Then they go out and change positions with the four outside players.

THOUGHTS

This practice looks at what happens when a midfielder is successful at breaking through the opposition's midfield and starts to attack the other team's defense. The attacks will come from various angles. What movements do the forwards make? And what effect does this have on the defensive team?

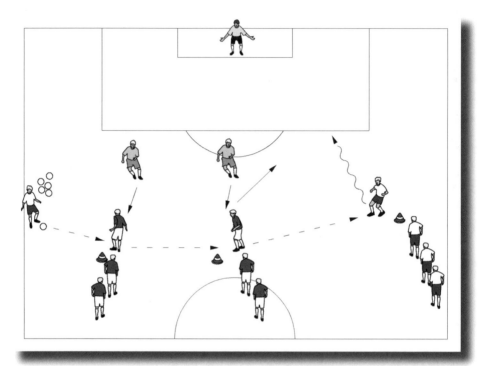

SET-UP

- 3 groups of 4 players: 2 groups act as attackers/defenders, 1 group acts as wide players.
- Attackers become defenders after each go. Each team has a period of time as the wide players.
- To start the practice the coach passes to one of the central attackers.

THOUGHTS

This situation happens regularly in both youth and senior soccer with players either not see-ing the wide player or delaying the pass and therefore losing the opportunity to score. The practice is set up in order to paint a picture in the players' minds of what to do. However, it is the player's choice whether to pass to the wide player or use him as a decoy. The defenders also have many choices to make. Do they pressure? Or sit back and try to cover the space in behind? Ideally, the ball will be switched to the wide player who runs and shoots or crosses for his teammates.

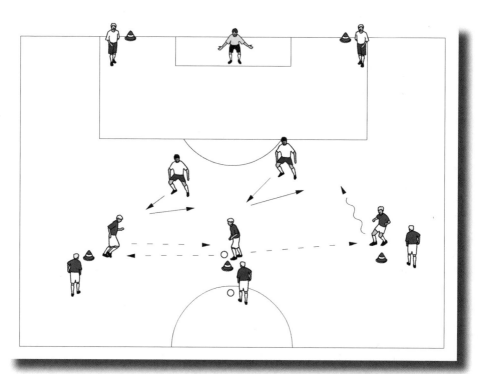

SET-UP

⊙ 5 stations, players move diagonally up and down into the next role/position after 5-7 mins.

⊙ To start, the three attackers pass to each other using a maximum of two touches. The defenders move across and take up good defensive positions in relation to the ball. On the coach's whistle the player in possession dribbles in the area to make a 3v2.

⊙ The sessions can be progressed in many ways by adding more defenders and a target striker. How do the defenders react to attacks from different angles? How do the attacking team change their priorities and movement actions?

THOUGHTS

This practice was designed to give the defenders more thought in how they should defend in regard to where the attack initially starts. Which way they show and what pressure they put on the attackers is also up for debate. The attackers also have to be bright and use various movements, overlaps and quick interchanges.

SET-UP

⊛ 5 stations as numbered in the diagram, [1] center back [2] center forward [3] right
   midfield [4] defensive midfield [5] left midfield

⊛ The coach passes into the center forward to start the practice. The wide players
   support and the attackers try to combine and score. The defensive center back tries
   to hold up play while the defensive midfielder makes a quick recovery run to help
   him defend.

THOUGHTS

This session forces players to make certain actions. For instance, the central attacker must
firstly hold up play and then pass to one of his supporting wide players. Then the attackers
must combine quickly and at match speed before the defensive midfielder recovers. Also, it
forces the central defender to try to delay the attackers and the defensive midfielder to react
and recover very quickly.

SET-UP

⊛ Three groups of four players: one group act as defenders, one group play down the left channel and one group down the right channel.

⊛ The first player on the left and right become the forwards and the next players the midfielders. The defenders have one player in each channel, another starts on the middle line and the other rests.

⊛ The practice starts with the coach passing to the midfielder or attacker in one of the channels. The middle defender can go in either channel to make a 2v2. The attackers try to score or switch the ball quickly to the other channel in order to make a 2v1. The middle defender is the only player that can go in both channels. The attackers can play back to the coach if they are blocked off.

⊛ The forwards rotate in their channel with the midfielder becoming a forward and then resting. The defenders rotate by starting in the left channel, then becoming the middle defender and then in the right channel before resting. Each group has a spell as the defenders.

THOUGHTS
This practice is set up to remind players that if we can quickly switch the ball from one side of the pitch to the other, we can take advantage of a 1v1 or 2v1 situation and also that if we are blocked off down one side then we need to turn back, be patient and attack the other side. After players are showing good decision making, take out the middle line of cones and attack just one goal with a normal pitch set up.

SET-UP

- ⊛ 4 players start in their own 15x10 yd area defending a small goal. One player starts in the middle zone with a ball.

- ⊛ The player in the middle zone can attack any of the four player's goals. If he is successful in scoring a goal or if the defender wins the ball, the middle player now stays in that area while the initial defender attacks any player he likes.

- ⊛ The practice continues for a set time. The player scoring the most goals is the winner.

> **THOUGHTS**
> This practice was designed to work continuously on 1v1 with the knowledge that if you defend well then you get the chance to attack the opposition's goal. The 1v1 situations become very realistic as the players try to compete and ultimately win the game.

SET-UP

- 5 groups of 3 players numbered 1 to 3: Four groups start in each 20x20 yard area with number 1 first acting as the keeper in a normal goal.
- The middle group attack any team they wish and try to make use of their overload and score. If they are successful or the defenders win the ball, the middle team stay in that area and the defending team come out to attack any team of their choice.
- The game continues for a set time with the team scoring the most goals declared the winners.

THOUGHTS

This is a progression from the previous practice but with additional players, real goals and now an overload. The practice focuses on the importance of taking advantage of an overload situation and scoring or the other team now have a chance to attack and score. Also teaches the lesson that defending well gives you the chance to attack and the reward of an overload situation.

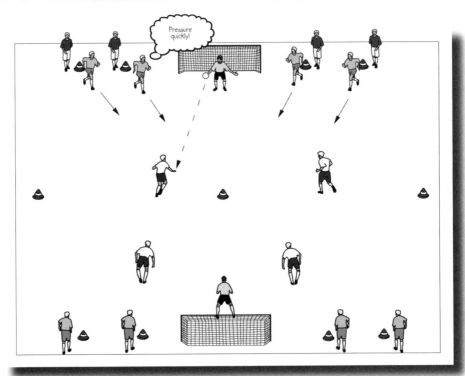

SET-UP

- 4 groups of 4 players, 1 team acts as the middle players for 5-7 minutes.
- To start the practice, the goalkeeper throws the ball out to the two yellow players. The four red defenders hunt together to win the ball back and then go to attack the two yellow defenders in the other half. If the two yellow defenders win back possession, they can play forward into the two yellow attackers who try to score.

THOUGHTS

Many young players run towards the ball and this drill can help in two key areas of play. Firstly it is important that we work in groups to hunt and win back possession. Secondly, once we have won possession, it is important that we spread out and make the pitch big but also that we don't all just race forward to score. The practice gives key hints to the players that they must work as a group to win the ball but what happens when we attack? Must all the players go into the attacking half? What happens if the yellow defenders win possession back and pass to their attackers who are now free to score? The questions will be answered.

SET-UP

- Two teams play 2v2 in the middle of the pitch, 8 players surround the pitch with a ball each

- To start the practice the coach calls out the name of one of the outside players who then passes a ball onto the pitch. The teams defend one goal and attack the other.

- The game lasts until all eight balls have been played; therefore there are eight opportunities to score. Two new teams enter the middle and play the next game.

THOUGHTS

This practice looks at how players react after a ball has left the field; do they switch on to the next ball? Or do they switch off and give the opposition an opportunity to score? The practice ensures real competition, especially as the number of balls to be played decreases. The practice can be used with any number of players in the middle zone.

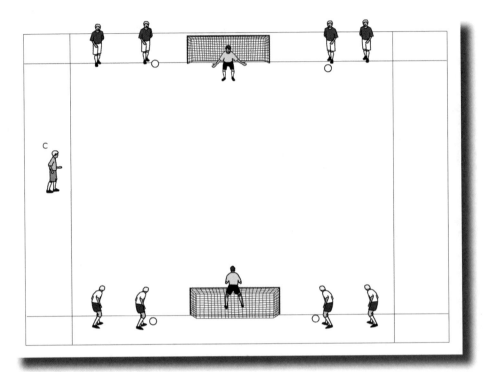

SET-UP

- Two teams line up by the side of their goal. Each team has two balls to attack with. On the coach's whistle the two teams attack each other's goal and continue to play until all four balls have been scored or left the pitch.

- The team scoring the most goals wins and then all players return and restart the practice.

THOUGHTS

The players love this practice as it gives them lots of different 1v1, 2v1 and 3v2 situations and many choices and decisions to make. When a goal is scored or a ball leaves play the players must react and affect what happens to another ball. The practice may seem like chaos at first but stick with it as after one or two goes the teams will start communicating and playing tactically with certain players choosing to defend whilst others attack.

SET-UP

⊛ 6 stations as shown in the diagram. Players move to the next station on their left after each go or spend 5-7 minutes at each station.

⊛ The defensive midfielder in position 1 starts with the ball and passes to any of the three attackers to start the practice. The three attackers try to play quickly and take advantage of their 3v2 overload before the defensive midfielder recovers. The two central defenders try to hold up the attackers until the midfielder recovers and makes the game a 3v3.

⊛ The ball must be passed to a different attacker in the next attack.

THOUGHTS

This practice was designed specifically to look at how quickly the midfielder recovers to help his defenders and how the defenders react and pressure in relation to where the ball is. The attackers also have various movements and options depending on who first receives the ball.

SET-UP

- 3 zones [two big end zones and a small middle "transition" zone]
- Starts with a 3v2 in one end zone with the defensive team trying to win back possession and passing into the player or players that have pulled off in the middle area. The player in the middle area receives, turns and dribbles to make a 3v2 at the other end.
- When defending, a team must have at least one and a maximum of two players that have pulled off into the middle 'transition" zone.
- PROGRESSION: Take away the zone and now encourage the players to pull off their marker. Give them the following insight: "If the defender comes tight, spin and receive into the space behind, if the defender stays in the same position, receive to feet".

THOUGHTS
Young players who play as wide or central attackers are often easily marked as they tend to stand right next to their markers. This practice tries to show them that any movement causes a problem for defenders and gives you a different option to receive.

SET-UP

- Two equal teams with two goals and 4 gates in the wide areas
- Coach calls out which game is to be played:
  Normal game – score in the two goals
  4 Goals – players try to dribble through the gates
  Keep ball – players try to get 6 passes for a goal

THOUGHTS

Simple game tactics that I use for my young players are to try and play through the middle, if blocked then try to play down the wings, if still blocked turn back and keep possession, then start the process again. This game is developed to work on these areas and test the players' awareness of what choice they should make. Eventually the coach can stop calling out the game to be played and just play with 6 passes counting as one goal, dribbling through the gates counting as one goal and two goals for scoring in the net. The team in possession now has three ways to score a goal and will find that scoring by dribbling or keeping possession often leads to a chance at scoring in the net.

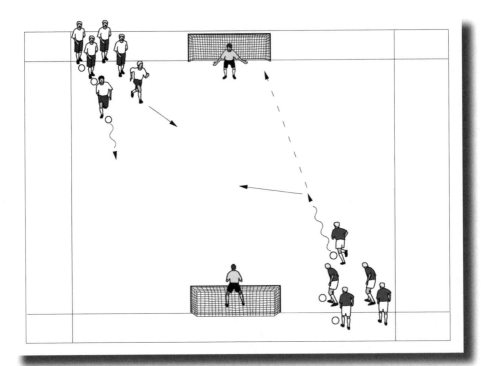

SET-UP

- Group of players with balls as shown in the diagram
- Once a ball has been scored or left play, the next players and ball enter the pitch.
- To start the practice a red player dribbles and has 3 touches to score;
  Then two yellows make it 2v1;
  Then two reds make it 3v2;
  Then two yellows make it 4v3;
  Then two reds make it 5v4;
  Then one yellow makes it a 5v5 game.
- There are 6 opportunities to score, then both teams mix up their order and now the yellow team starts first.

> **THOUGHTS**
> The team that wins this game will be the one that makes use of the spare player the best. This simple practice is a mirror of what actually happens in a real match. If the players can appreciate how important these overloads are, then the group will have greater success in matches.

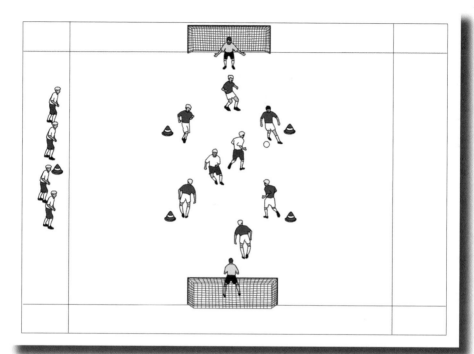

SET-UP

- ◉ The red team defend first. Four players go into the 10x10 yard area while one defender goes into each end zone

- ◉ The yellow team work in pairs with the first pair going into the 10x10 yard area. The other pairs wait and enter for the next attack

- ◉ The four red players start by trying to keep possession. If they can make ten passes they get a goal and eject the two yellow players out, but if the yellow players force a mistake and win possession they are free to attack one of the end zones and make a 2v1 to finish.

- ◉ The reds rotate their middle and end zone players regularly. The yellow pairs have two goes each before the teams switch roles. The team with the most goals wins the game.

THOUGHTS

The practice is set up to get players working hard to win the ball back and then seeing the rewards of the hard work by getting a 2v1 to attack. It also shows the team keeping possession the value of having the ball and making good use of their possession.

SET-UP

- Three teams of four players. Two teams play while one team acts as rebound players on the outside.
- Each team defends two goals and attacks two. In possession the players have an 8v4 as they can play wall passes with the outside players who have 2 touches to pass back into play.

THOUGHTS

This session is used to work on 1-2's and supporting runs to receive a pass. The players don't have to play out but I often include a rule that if the players score with I touch from an outside pass then they get two goals. This gives the players an extra incentive to support and look for quick wall passes.

SET-UP

- 6 stations, after each go the players move to the left and wait in line to play the next role/position in the practice.
- To start the practice, the central attacker dribbles at the center back, the wide players make supporting runs and the two defensive full backs try to recover.

THOUGHTS

This situation occurs often in mini-soccer with the player in possession regularly making the wrong decision or delaying the speed of the attack and allowing the defenders to recover. This practice forces the attackers to play at speed with positive decisions being made in order to successfully get a shot at goal. If run properly, this session should work with non-bib and bib players in a contest to defend well in one go before having a chance to attack in the next turn. I have run this session in a competition with scores being counted. The defenders then play with match tempo and try to defend, knowing that if they do they can take the lead by scoring in the next attack.

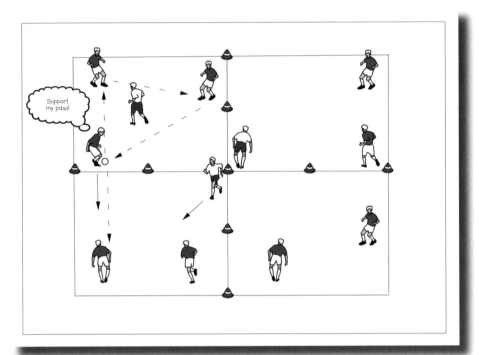

SET-UP

⊛ Four 10x10 yard areas

⊛ 12 players. 3 players act as defenders and start on the middle cone. 3 squares have 2 attackers and one square has 3 attackers and a ball.

⊛ To start, the first defender goes into the area with three attackers to defend. The attackers try to make three passes and then transfer the ball to another square. The player who passes to the other square must support his pass and make three players in the next square. The original defender runs back to the middle and the next defender goes in to pressure the ball

THOUGHTS

This practice is designed to work on passing and supporting. The area is small and the players need to show good composure. The aim is to make the space to pass longer and then support the pass. The defenders have to work hard to stop the attackers and see how many mistakes they can force in a set time.

SET-UP

- Two equal teams and two goalkeepers [can play without keepers]

- To start, both teams have one ball each and are on the field. To get the players in the theme of quick passing the coach should set the teams challenges such as the first team to make 20 passes, then 30 passes and finally 50 passes. This drill will get the players warmed up nicely

- Then one of the teams should go to the outside. The team left in the middle passes unopposed until the coach calls the other team to enter the field. The team entering has 30 seconds to win possession and score in one of the two goals. If the team in possession mange to last the 30 seconds then they are the ones who get the goal.

THOUGHTS

This practice asks many questions of both teams. The team in possession are under strong pressure from the opposition who are desperate to win the ball. Can they protect possession and stay relaxed and composed in a pressured situation? Do the team hunting possession work as a group? Do they make good decisions when winning the ball back or do they rush and give possession back to their opponents?

SET-UP

- Four areas: [1] keep away [2] head tennis [3] 2v2 game [4] goalkeeper wars
- Groups of 4 players, #'s 1 to 4. Player 1 is the captain and organizer of the group
- **Pitch 1** – 3v1 keep away. Player 1 starts in the middle and passes the bib to the player he wins possession from or who makes a mistake

  Pitch 2 – Head tennis. Player 1 partners with player 2 and they play with 3 touches per player and one bounce allowed

  Pitch 3 – 2v2 game. Player 1 partners with Player 3 in this game, which is a normal game with no keepers

  Pitch 4 – Goalkeeper wars. Player 1 partners with player 4 and the rules are that each team has a shot in their own half to try and score against two keepers

---

THOUGHTS

This is a competitive circuit working on technique. Pitch 1 looks at passing, pitch 2 looks at control, pitch 3 works on skills and combination play and pitch 4 works on striking of the ball. Players should spend 3-5 minutes at each pitch before moving on.

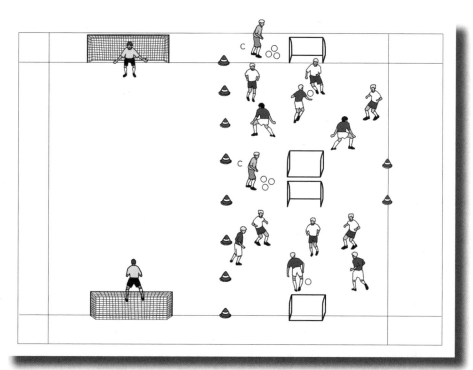

SET-UP

- Two teams of 6 players, each split in half to make two teams of three.
- The teams play 3v3 games until the coach calls out and the players quickly race onto the big pitch to play 6v6.
- The coach places balls in the middle of the two 3v3 pitches and on his call the players race back onto the small pitches and continue the small games.

THOUGHTS

This practice allows for both the intensity of a small sided possession game and the player enjoyment of a normal game. It also works on reactions and has conditioning elements as the players race between pitches in order to get to the ball first and gain possession for their team.

SET-UP

- ⊛ Four goals placed as shown in the diagram
- ⊛ Three teams of four players, one team acts as keepers, one as forwards and one as defenders
- ⊛ On the coach's whistle the forwards play a 1v1 with the defender and try to score. If they score or the defender wins the ball, the player moves to the next pitch and waits for the coach's whistle to play again.
- ⊛ The forwards have 16 chances to score. After all the balls have been played the team counts up all the goals scored, rotates to a new role and the next team tries to beat their score.

THOUGHTS

This is a fun way to work on 1v1s as all the players are involved in the session and all have a reason to do well. The attackers are trying to score as many goals as possible while the defenders and keepers are trying to stop them and give their own teams a better chance of winning.

SET-UP

- Three groups of three players and one keeper as shown in the diagram
- To start, the defenders just put passive pressure on the attackers who bounce the ball back to the coach. On the fourth pass the game becomes live with the attackers trying to score.
- The coach passes to the three attackers one after the other. The defenders must pressure quickly and all take up good, realistic covering positions. On the fourth pass the coach passes to any of the attackers who then try to score. The attacking team can play back to the coach as many times as they like.
- After a turn as the attackers the team work as defenders before resting.

THOUGHTS

This practice is designed to look at the midfield or defensive three. The session forces the players to pressure quickly and the whole group to take up good support and cover positions. The aim is to firstly stop the attackers turning and then to win possession.

SET-UP

- Groups of three players and a keeper as shown in the diagram
- The keeper throws out to the defender to start, the attackers then pressure and try to win the ball and score. The defenders try to pass their way out of defense and run the ball out of the area in order to score.
- After a turn as the attackers, the team has a go as defenders before resting.

THOUGHTS

This practice is designed to work on the wide and central attackers pressuring high up the pitch with the knowledge that if they win the ball back they will have a good chance to score. The game will bring up certain questions and key learning factors for the pressing players such as: Do they pressure as a group? Do they pressure a back pass on the keeper? Must they always try to tackle or instead just block up the passing options?

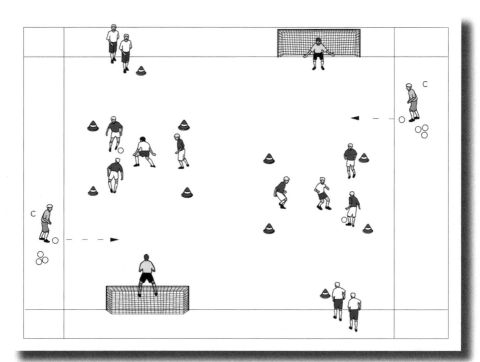

SET-UP

⊛ Two teams of six players, two keepers and two coaches/servers as shown

⊛ One team act as passers and one team act as defenders. The passers work in groups of three and the defenders work alone and have one turn in each area.

⊛ To start, the three players keep possession. If the three players can make ten passes they eject the defender and a new one enters the area. However, if the defender wins the ball or forces a mistake, the coach feeds the player a ball for a first time shot against the keeper.

⊛ Each defender has two goes in the middle, therefore the defending team has 12 chances to score. The teams then rotate and the team with the most goals at the end wins the game.

THOUGHTS

The game is designed to give realistic pressure and competition in a 3v1 possession game. The game also gives the defender the knowledge that by working hard and winning possession he is rewarded with a chance to attack.

SET-UP

- Three groups of four players and one keeper as shown in the diagram.
- One group work as defenders, one group work as attackers and one group work as passers/receivers. Teams rotate after a set time.
- To start, the top passer at the edge of the box passes back to his teammate. This is the signal for the defender to pressure and stop him turning. The passer then returns the pass back to his teammate. The defender now pressures him and shows the player inside or outside. The coach now passes to the two attackers, and now both defenders work together to try to stop the attackers scoring in a 2v2 situation.

THOUGHTS

This game is used to develop various defending principles. The game is fun but also demanding on the players as they have to pressure quickly and show realistic body positions and pressure distances. The three areas of the session look at different situations in a game and how players react.

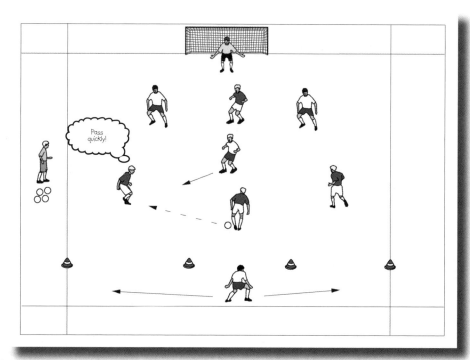

SET-UP

⊚ Two teams of four players and a keeper as shown in the diagram.

⊚ The defending team start with three defenders in the area and a target player at the top of the area. The attacking team have all four players in the attacking area.

⊚ To start the practice the coach passes to the attacking team who try to use their over-load to score. The defending team try to win possession and play to their target man. If the defenders are able to pass to their target man, he dribbles into the area and the teams reverse roles with the attackers now defending and having to send a player as a target. The teams automatically reverse roles if the attacking team have a shot that goes wide or the defending team force the attackers to make a pass out of the area.

THOUGHTS

The game is very fast with lots of changes from being attackers to defenders, which makes it demanding on the players. The harder the players work the more they start to appreciate being attackers and having control of the ball and a spare man. This practice also gives the attackers real game pressure as a poor pass or miss-placed shot loses them their chance to attack and now they must defend.

SET-UP

- Three groups of four players. Two groups work together and try to keep possessions, one group work as defenders. The area is set up as shown in the diagram with four small goals.
- The team with eight players try to keep possession, counting the number of passes. The four defending players try to win the ball and score quickly in any of the four goals. The aim is to complete the biggest set of passes possible
- The teams all rotate after a set time and all have a go as the defenders.

THOUGHTS

A key tactic of the teams I coach is that once we win possession back we must make a set of passes in order to allow us to get our shape back, give us control of the game and another chance to attack. The players have to understand is impossible to go for the knockout blow and score on every possession, therefore we must rest and keep the ball. I often give the team a scenario that we are 1-0 up in the last minute of a cup final, keep possession and become champions.

SET-UP

- Two teams of five players and two goals as shown in the diagram.

- One team act as defenders with three players in defense and two players as keepers. The attacking team have five players spread out across the pitch.

- The coach passes to the five attackers who try to use their overload advantage in order to score in either of the goals. If the attacking team lose possession, shoot wide, have a shot saved or pass out of the area then they must let the defending team dribble and pass to the coach and both teams reverse roles.

> **THOUGHTS**
>
> This practice places a big emphasis on making sure you take advantage of a good overload position. Five outfield players against three defenders should see lots of goal action and quick movement of the ball. The defending team will have to work to their maximum in order to force a mistake. The pitch should be reasonably small in order to force the attacking team to pass with high intensity.

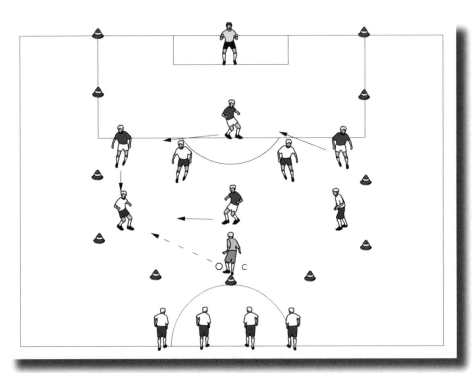

SET-UP

- Three teams of four players and one keeper as shown in the diagram.
- One team acts as defenders, one team as attackers and one team rests.
- The coach passes to the attacker to start the practice. The attackers try to build up and score. If the attackers score they get another ball from the coach and attempt to score again. The game is played with real throw-ins and corner kicks/free kicks. The only way the defenders get out is by passing to the coach/target player. The attacking team can play back to the coach if needed.
- Attackers become defenders, defenders then rest. The team with the most goals after a set time is the winners.

THOUGHTS

This practice works both the defenders and the attackers. The competition between the three teams ensures real game tempo and intensity. The teams must take advantage of their attacking role and score as many goals as possible or they know they will have to defend and face the prospect of going behind in the game.

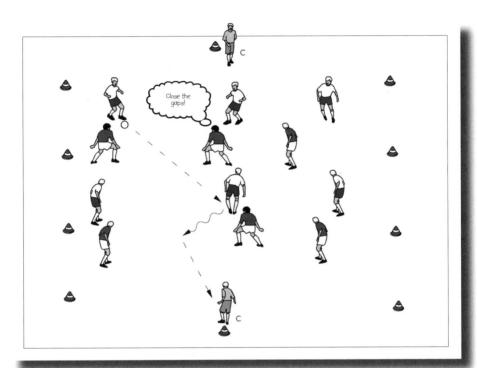

SET-UP

- Two teams of six players and two target players/coaches. The teams split into two groups of three players and are set up as shown in the diagram.

- The coach passes to the first attacking team who try to combine and pass through to their teammates. If successful their teammates now turn and try to play through to the coach in order to gain a goal. The coach should move across the end line in order to receive. The defending team must try to stop this by closing the gaps and working across to support/cover each other. One of the defenders can break out and pressure the player in possession but this must be only one player at a time.

THOUGHTS
This game was designed to look at the midfield and defense stopping balls through to the opposition's attackers and then stopping the attackers getting a shot at goal. The midfield must stop the ball being played through by showing good cover and pressure on the ball. If the ball is played through, one of the defenders should pressure the attacker who receives and stop him from turning and therefore forcing him back to his defense.

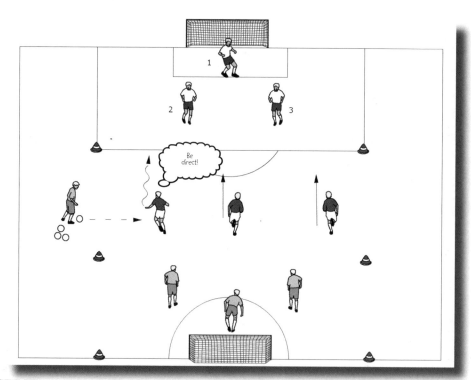

SET-UP

- Three teams of three players as shown in the diagram.
- Each team number themselves 1-3 and take turns at being the keeper.
- To start the practice the coach passes to the team in the middle who attack one of the end zones and try to score in a 3v2 situation. If the team are successful and score, they turn and receive another ball from the coach and attack the other goal. If the attackers shoot wide, have a shot saved or the defenders win possession, the roles are reversed and they come out of defense to receive a pass and attack the other goal.

THOUGHTS

This practice is a fast paced game with lots of overload and goal scoring situations. The teams learn that when attacking they must make use of their spare player and when defending, if they work hard and defend well, they will get a chance to attack and score at the other end.

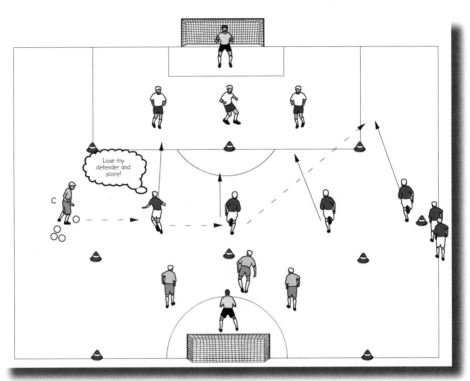

SET-UP

- ⊛ Four teams of three players and two keepers.

- ⊛ The coach passes to the team in the middle zone who have to make two passes before playing out to the wide player who crosses for the players to attack in a 3v3 situation. Once the cross has been made the game continues until a goal is scored or the ball leaves play. If the attackers manage to score then they turn, receive another pass from the coach and combine to attack the other goal however, if the defenders stop them scoring then the roles are reversed and they come out of the zone to receive a pass from the coach.

- ⊛ The game is played in four 5 minute sections with each team taking a turn as the wide players. The team with the most goals is declared the winners.

THOUGHTS

This practices progresses from the 3v2 counter game and now looks at how teams both defend and attack from crosses. The practice also looks at quick combination play in the build up in order to get a ball wide. The game is fast paced with lots of action and fun as all the players have an active role in the game.

SET-UP

- Two teams of equal players and a keeper, set us as shown in the diagram. The first two players on each team go out to make the first defenders and attackers.

- The coach starts by declaring which team is going to attack first. The coach then passes to the first player on the attacking team who now dribbles to make a 3v2. The first player on the defending team must run, touch the flag/pole before turning and sprinting to recover.

- The players who have dribbled/run back stay in for the next two attacks before joining the back of their lines and waiting another turn. Therefore, all players have a chance to be the player dribbling in, the recovering defender, the central attacker and the central defender.

- The coach starts the next attack by passing the ball to the team that defended the previous attack. Each time the roles reverse and the teams compete to score the most goals.

THOUGHTS

This practice is a competition between the two teams. The team must attack or defend well in order to give themselves the chance to win the game. This gives the practice a real competitive edge that ensures real game tempo and concentration from all the players. The resting players constantly encourage teammates to do well as they defend or attack for the team.

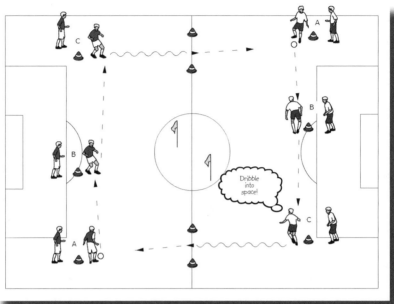

SET-UP ▬▬▬▬▬

⊛ Six stations, two gates and two poles/mannequins acting as defenders.

⊛ To start the practice, both players on station A pass inside and follow. The center player at station B opens out and switches play quickly to the player at station C, who receives and dribbles at pace through the gate. Once through the gate he passes to the next player at station A.

⊛ When a player has dribbled through the gate and passes, he then pressures the player at station A, forcing him into passing quickly and accurately inside to the player at station B. The flag/pole is in the position of an opposing player and the center player at station B must quickly switch play in order for the team to advance and make use of the space created.

THOUGHTS

This practice develops the team's ability to switch play quickly and then take advantage of the space created by dribbling quickly into an advanced position. Many teams do not show enough care when switching the ball in this type of situation and have too many touches or play slow passes that allow the opposition to slide across and shut down the options. Therefore it is essential for the coach to ensure the players receive the ball correctly and that they play passes with both proper weight and accuracy. Also, the player receiving the ball from the switched pass must be positive and take a first touch into the space before accelerating forward.

SET-UP

- Eight stations, two gates and two mannequins/poles acting as defenders.

- The player at station A is now being blocked from playing inside to the center player by a defender/flag. Therefore, he needs to play forward into his midfielder/ forward who receives and sets back to the center player who has moved into a good position to receive. The center player then switches play to the player at station D who accelerates forward and through the gate to pass.

- After passing, the player again pressures the player at station A and forces him inside.

THOUGHTS

This practice progresses nicely from the previous one and uses a center midfielder/forward to bounce the ball off in order to switch play. This gives the team valuable knowledge and enables them to problem-solve quickly by assessing their options in relation to how the opposition choose to pressure.

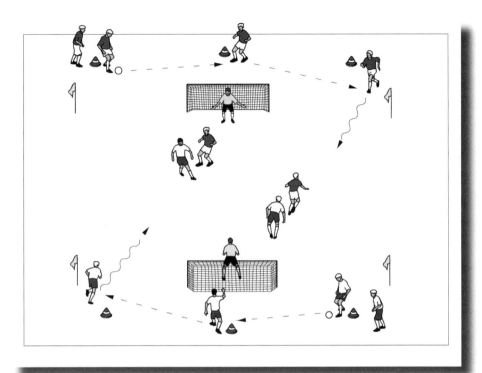

SET-UP

- Six stations, two goals and two keepers.
- This time when the players switch the ball and the final player dribbles forward to attack he is now heading for goal and breaking forward to make a 2v1 situation.
- After each pass you move up a station. After being the player that dribbles forward you become the attacker in the box and then the defender before joining the back of the opposite line. The defender in this practice only holds the bib to ensure quick switching of roles.

THOUGHTS

This progression moves the practice into a game situation where the players now see the advantage of switching play quickly in order to gain a 2v1 situation and the opportunity to score a goal. I have run this practice with the rule that the team must get a shot on goal within 12 seconds of the first pass, which ensures the team play at the correct tempo required in a match. A simple progression to this drill is to add another defender and attacker to make a 3v2 situation.

SET-UP

⊛ A goalkeeper, 4 defenders, 4 attackers and three target goals.

⊛ To start the practice the attacking wide players and midfielder drop off to allow the keeper to throw out to one of his full backs. The attackers then press quickly in order to stop the defenders playing forward and then win the ball back in order to attack and score.

THOUGHTS

This practice enables a coach to get across his thoughts and ideas on how the team will defend in the final third. The practice can be modified to suit any formation; the set up in the diagram is for 8v8 and shows my own preference in this situation. I ask my wide players to drop off and force the opposition to play out from defense. Once the keeper passes to one of his full backs the forward's job is to keep play on that side of the pitch, the next job is for the wide player to pressure quickly and stop any passes going outside him, therefore forcing the full back inside. The center midfielder now comes inside of his marker to stop both the pass into the forwards and the pass to the opposition's midfielder. Finally the opposite wide player tucks in to again ensure no pass is played in to midfield. I give my players the knowledge that the player receiving possession will only have 1 second to make his mind up and pass before we tackle him in an advanced position and go on to have a chance to score.

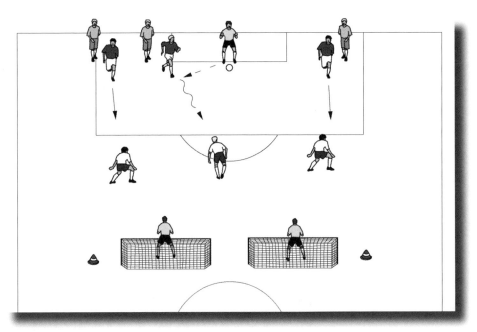

SET-UP

- 3 goals, 3 keepers and 3 teams of players.
- To start the practice the keeper roles out to one of his teammates. The player must be as direct as possible by dribbling directly at the opposition's defense and by combining with his teammates in order to score in one of the two goals.
- After having a turn as the attackers the team then stay on the pitch and act as the defenders in the next attack

THOUGHTS

This practice looks at direct dribbling play from the three attackers. The player in possession has a one on one situation and is attacking two goals, therefore he has plenty of space and directions to attack. The attacker's teams mate must make supporting runs and overlaps in order to disrupt the defending players and try to isolate the player in a 1v1 situation whilst also being in a good position to receive a pass. If the defenders win the ball back they can attack the opposite goal and now the attackers must transfer their thoughts into winning the ball back and attacking once again.

SET-UP

⊛ One keeper, three stations [left side, right side, attack/defenders]

⊛ To start, the central player passes wide to his teammate and overlaps.
    The wide player dribbles inside to attack the two defenders in a 3v2 situation.

⊛ The attackers rotate from the left to the right with the overlapping player becoming
    the wide player in the next attack. The attacker and defenders have a bib and rotate
    who holds the bib and therefore works as the attacker.

THOUGHTS

This practice looks at a midfielder passing wide and then making a supporting overlap. The wide
player must dribble at pace inside and towards the defenders in order to allow this to happen.
Also the center attacker must try to pull away and into space as this will give the defenders a
problem and either pull them apart to enable a 2v1 situation or together to allow a pass wide and
behind them. The speed of the attack must be quick and realistic with the rule that an attempt
on goal must be made within a certain time limit.

SET-UP

- One keeper, four stations and twelve players.
- To start, both forwards pull of their markers. The coach chooses which forward to pass to, and immediately the wide player on that side of the pitch makes a forward run on the outside of his teammate. The forward turns and dribbles to make a 3v2. The other forward must now react and make a run into an advanced attacking position.
- The wide player making an attacking run stays on the pitch for the next attack and replaces the forward who received the initial pass

---

THOUGHTS

This practice looks at what happens when a forward comes short to receive the ball from his center midfielder. The opposition defender has a decision to make: Does he go with him and risk a pass in behind for the wide player to run onto? Or does he stay in his position and allow the forward to receive and turn? I personally feel that he will likely hold his position, but the split second of hesitation or uncertainty can be crucial and either way the attacking team should gain an advantage. It's important that the players see the choices available to them and act quickly in order to get a chance to score.

SET-UP

- A keeper and ten players who work in pairs and spread out across the five stations as shown in the diagram
- To start, the central attacker must pass to one of his wide players and then overlap him. The three attackers then try to attack and score while the defenders react and work together to stop them scoring.
- After a set time the players rotate and work at another station.

THOUGHTS

The session looks at overlapping in the final thirds of the pitch and the options/decisions it gives the player in possession and the attacking team. The overlap will cause some uncertainty in the two defending players and the pace at which the attackers play will often determine whether they have enough time to adjust. Therefore, the attackers must act quickly by using the overlap with a through pass or as a decoy for the player in possession to switch play or go alone

SET-UP

○ 5 stations: A,B,C,D,E. Two players at each station [one from each team] and a keeper as shown in the diagram.

○ The players spend 3-5 minutes repeating the same role before moving to the next station in alphabetical order.

○ To start, the central attacker dribbles towards the opposition's goal. He has three choices:

1 pass to the supporting player on the left
2 pass to the supporting player on the right
3 use the supporting players as a decoy and dribble to shoot.

The next attack will see the other team now having the advantage

---

THOUGHTS

This practice is designed to improve quick decisions and decisive play in and around the area and also to enhance the belief of playing with good width and natural wide players. If the two wide players hold their wide position it gives the two defenders many problems to solve.

SET-UP

- Three groups of four players and a keeper as shown in the diagram.
- The defending group have two roles to play: as a center back and then as the center midfielder before resting. To start the practice the center back passes to the center midfielder who tries to turn and score in the small goal. The two attacking midfielders must pressure quickly, win possession and break forward for a 2v1 to finish.
- After a set time the teams rotate

THOUGHTS
This practice is set up to work on the midfielders pressing quickly to stop players turning and hunting in groups to win the ball. Once the team have won possession the practice then focuses on what happens next by forcing them to attack quickly in order to get a goal scoring opportunity.

FINISHING PRACTICES

"
They call it coaching, but it's teaching, you don't just
tell them what to do, you show them.
"

Finishing practices

Scoring goals is the ultimate aim of soccer and to score goals in a real match, players have to use skill, imagination, creativity, awareness, pace and strength in order to convert their chances. Therefore finishing sessions must develop these qualities.

The following practices were created with the goal to inspire players while giving them different problems to solve. The players have to play under pressure, they have to react to different types of service and have choices to make on different techniques to use and whether they should shoot early or combine with a teammate.

All the practices run quickly and with sharp movements, there are no long queues waiting to shoot and every player has a role and function to complete in order for the practice to run smoothly.

FINISHING PRACTICES

SESSION	TITLE
1.	4 PLAYER SHOOTOUT
2.	4 PLAYER, SKILL SHOOTOUT
3.	QUICK TOUCH AND STRIKE
4.	QUICK TOUCH AND STRIKE –PROGRESSION
5.	REACTION FINISHING
6.	REACTION FINISHING –PROGRESSION 1
7.	REACTION FINISHING –PROGRESSION 2
8.	REACTION FINISHING –PROGRESSION 3
9.	TARGET MAN
10.	ONE-TWO AND FINISH
11.	WIDE PLAYER MOVEMENT TO RECEIVE
12.	CENTRE MIDFIELD, SUPPORTING RUN
13.	TWO TEAM REACTION, CROSSING PRACTICE
14.	KING OF THE PENALTY AREA
15.	DRIBBLE, TAKE AND FINISH
16.	LOSE YOUR MARKER
17.	LOSE YOUR MARKER –PROGRESSION 1
18.	MOVEMENTS TO SCORE
19.	MOVEMENTS TO SCORE –PROGRESSION 1
20.	MOVEMENTS TO SCORE –PROGRESSION 2
21.	PLAYING WITH YOUR BACK TO GOAL
22.	PLAYING WITH YOUR BACK TO GOAL –PROGRESSION 1
23.	PLAYING WITH YOUR BACK TO GOAL –PROGRESSION 2
24.	SCORING IN A CROWDED BOX
25.	SCORING IN A CROWDED BOX –PROGRESSION 1
26.	FINISHING CIRCUIT
27.	ATTACKER V DEFENDER CIRCUIT
28.	VOLLEY, ONE-TWO AND STRIKE
29.	FINISHING AT SPEED CIRCUIT
30.	TEAM BUILD UP TO CROSS AND SCORE
31.	WIDE PLAYER GOES INSIDE OR OUTSIDE TO CROSS
32.	3 CHANCES TO SCORE
33.	TAKING THE BALL OUT OF THE AIR TO FINISH
34.	CUTTING ACROSS THE DEFENDER TO SHOOT
35.	CONTROLLING A BALL OUT OF THE AIR TO SCORE
36.	A.B.C FINISHING
37.	MIDFIELDERS FINISHING CIRCUIT
38.	ATTACKING MIDFIELDER, GETTING PAST THE STRIKER TO SCORE
39.	DEFENDER V ATTACKER CIRCUIT
40.	SCORING FROM A CUT BACK
41.	CROSSING ALLEY 2v1
42.	QUICK FINSIHING AROUND THE BOX
43.	BEATING DEFENDERS ON THE INSIDE AND OUTSIDE TO FINISH
44.	PASS,SET,SPIN AND FINISH
45.	FORWARD GETTING BACK ONSIDE TO FINISH
46.	ONE-TWO COMBINATION TO FINISH
47.	WIDE PLAYER COMING INSIDE
48.	1v1 DRIBBLING WITH DANGER
49.	OPENING OUT IN ORDER TO CROSS AND FINISH
50.	ONE TOUCH COMBINATIONS
51.	ONE TOUCH COMBINATIONS –PROGRESSION 1
52.	ONE TOUCH COMBINATIONS –PROGRESSION 2
53.	ONE TOUCH COMBINATIONS –PROGRESSION 3
54.	FINISHING OUTSIDE THE BOX

55.	LETTING THE BALL RUN ACROSS YOUR BODY TO SHOOT
56.	DEFENDING YOUR AREA
57.	WIDE PLAY
58.	WIDE PLAYER INSIDE, FORWARD BENDING HIS RUN
59.	ATTACKING PASSING OPTIONS
60.	QUICK COUNTER
61.	PITCH SMALL IN DEFENCE, BIG IN ATTACK
62.	MIDFIELD SUPPORTING OF TARGET MAN
63.	MIDFIELD SUPPORTING OF TARGET MAN –PROGRESSION 1
64.	CROSSING EARLY OR GETTNG TO THE BY-LINE
65.	FORWARDS MOVEMENT TO RECEIVE AND REACTION TO 2ND PASS
66.	FORWARDS MOVEMENT TO RECEIVE–PROGRESSION 1
67.	FORWARD COMING SHORT AND GETTING INVOLVED WITH THE BUILD UP
68.	FORWARD COMING SHORT AND GETTING INVOLVED –PROGRESSION 1
69.	WIDE PLAYER MAKING A RUN OFF THE LINE POSITION
70.	ATTACKING A LOW, DRIVEN CROSS
71.	QUICK PASSING GIVES US A CHANCE TO DRIBBLE
72.	FORWARDS MOVEMENT TO SCORE FROM A THROUGH PASS
73.	OVERLAPPING IN WIDE AREAS
74.	CUTTING ACROSS A DEFENDER TO SCORE
75.	TEAM FINISHING BATTLES
76.	POWER FROM DISTANCE, PLACEMENT IN THE BOX
77.	FIRST TOUCH GIVING YOU AN OPPORTUNITY TO SCORE
78.	FIRST TOUCH ACROSS YOUR BODY TO SCORE
79.	TEAM BUILD UP TO FINISH
80.	CONTROLLING AN AERIAL PASS AND SCORING
81.	LOSING A TIGHT MARKER AND ACCELERATING AWAY TO SCORE
82.	CENTRE MIDFIELDER PASSING TO MAKE SPACE TO ATTACK
83.	TEAM OPEN OUT AND THROUGH PASS TO FINISH
84.	OPENING BODY TO FINISH ACROSS GOAL
85.	FINISHING FROM CROSSES, ROLE REVERSAL GAME
86.	1v1 BATTLE TO SCORE
87.	TEAM BUILD UP TO CROSS AND SCORE
88.	TEAM BUILD UP TO CROSS AND SCORE –PROGRESSION 1

4 PLAYER SHOOTOUT

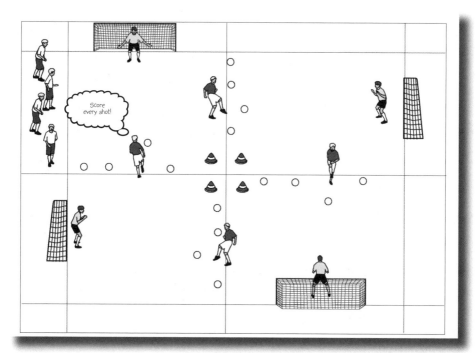

SET-UP

⊛ 12 players, four goals and 16 balls [can work with less players and balls if needed]

⊛ The pitch is set up as shown in the diagram. One team of four players work as shooters, one team as keepers while one team work as counters and are assigned to one player each.

⊛ On the coach's call, the players shoot at goal and race to the next goal to shoot. Once each player has had four shots, they race to get into the center square.

⊛ Players get 1 point for each goal and an extra point if they are the first into the center square. The four shooters are competing against each other to be the winner.

THOUGHTS

This practice is designed to work on speed and finishing at the same time. The players enjoy this practice as they are competing against the other shooters and therefore have to work at top speed without neglecting their technique and concentration when shooting. You can reduce the number of balls, goals and players depending on the size of your group.

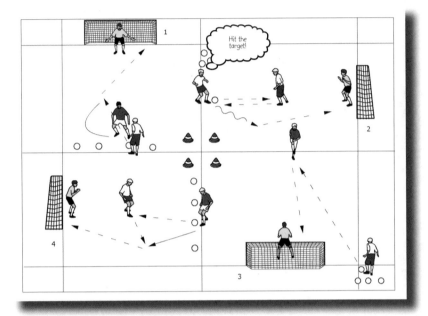

SET-UP

⊚ 12 players, 4 goals and 16 balls.

⊚ One team of four players act as shooters, one team as act as keepers and one team act as servers.

⊚ The four shooters compete against each other to see who scores the most goals.

⊚ At goal number 1 the server plays through the shooter's legs for a turn and finish. At goal 2 the shooter plays a pass to the server who returns the ball and pressures the shooter to have a touch to the side and shoot. At goal 3 the server passes a ball from the goal line for a first time strike. At goal 4 the shooter plays a one-two with the server and shoots.

⊚ The players wait for the coach's to call to shoot at each station, therefore all four players are working simultaneously.

THOUGHTS

This session looks at four different skills to finish and gives the shooters a variety of tech-niques to use. The practice uses all 12 players at the same time with all players playing an important role in the drill. The players enjoy this practice as once again it is competitive and has variation. You can reduce the number of goals used and shots taken if needed.

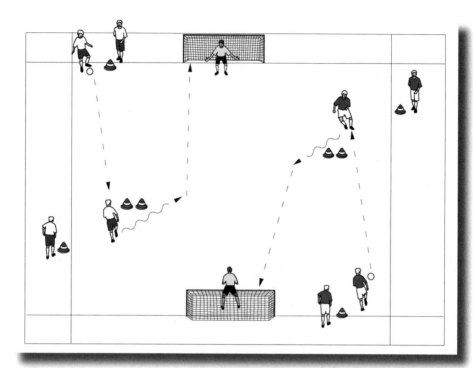

SET-UP

- Two groups of players, split up as shooters and passes, as shown in the diagram.
- To start the practice a pass is made down the side of the pitch, the receiving players has a touch inside the flag/cone and shoots quickly. The passer follows his pass and now becomes a shooter while the shooter collects his ball from goal and becomes a passer.

- The next pass can be made once the previous shot has been taken, this ensures a good tempo with lots of shots and minimal waiting time.

> **THOUGHTS**
> This practice is used to work on quick, sharp finishing. The players will learn how important their first touch is to the final shot as they are only allowed one touch before shooting. I always encourage disguise and variation in their shooting technique in order to wrong foot the keeper.

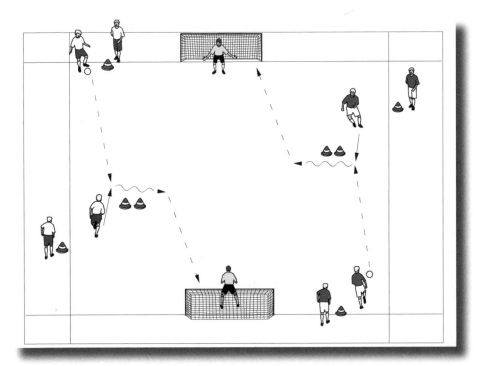

SET-UP

- This time the players have to race in front of the flag/cone in order to receive the ball. The players have one touch to turn and shoot as quickly as possible.
- After passing, the player becomes a shooter while the shooter gets his ball and becomes a passer going the other way.

THOUGHTS

This practice progresses nicely from the previous one but now with the emphasis on turning quickly to shoot. Often young players receive the ball in the box and try something impossible in order to shoot. I encourage my players to act simply and sharply by turning in one touch and striking the ball as early as possible. I ask them to visualize the keeper being unsighted with the ball going through the defender's legs or taking a deflection on its way to goal. This scenario happens frequently in top level matches.

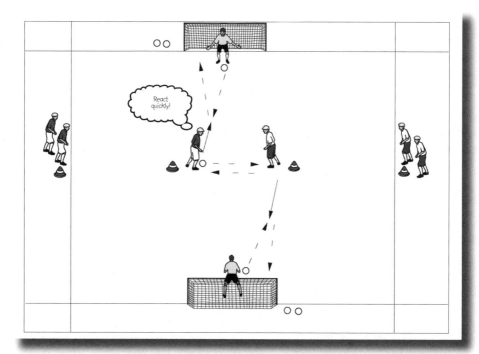

SET-UP

⊙   Two keepers, two goals, three balls and two teams. Set up as shown in the diagram.

⊙   The first two players come out to the center and pass a ball back and forth using one touch. The keepers have a ball in their hands ready to serve. One the coach's call of "left" or "right", the players leave the middle ball, turn and sprint, receive a serve from the keepers and then finish with a side foot from 10 yards. After serving the keepers react and try to save the shot.

> **THOUGHTS**
> This practice works on quick reaction from both the shooting players and the keepers. Can the players react quickly to the coach's call and finish with good power and disguise? The keepers must react as if their initial roll-out is actually a parried or rebounded shot. The shooters receive one point for scoring and an extra point for being the quickest player to score.

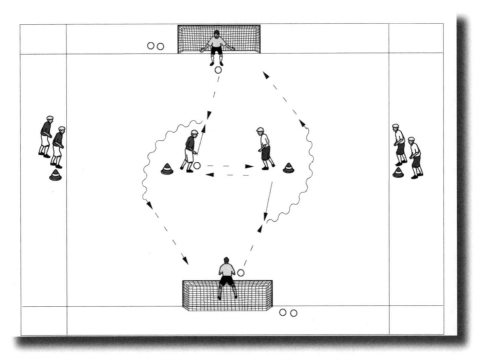

SET-UP

- ⊛   Same as previous practice as shown in the diagram.
- ⊛   The players now wait for the coach's call, sprint to receive a serve from the keepers but this time immediately turn to score in the opposite goal.

THOUGHTS

This progresses well from the previous practice. The players are now encouraged to use various turns in order to set themselves up to score. The players can now use a variation of techniques to finish [power, curved, side foot] in order to score and once again receive one point for scoring and an extra point for being the quickest to score.

SET-UP

⊛ This time the players have a ball each and the keepers now just fully concentrate on saving the shot.

⊛ Players face away from the goal they are going to shoot at and on the coach's call they roll their ball out of their feet, then quickly turn and shoot with the other player's ball. Once again the players receive one point for scoring a goal and an extra point for being the first to score.

THOUGHTS

This practice looks at player's ability to turn and his decision on whether to take another touch or to shoot first time. I ask my players to visualize the pass as a flick down or a through ball from a teammate. The players are encouraged to use sharp movements and disguise in order to catch the keepers by surprise or wrong-footed.

SET-UP

- This time the practice uses only one ball and is set up as shown in the diagram.
- The two players pass the ball back and forth using one touch. On the coach's call, the player in possession decides to attack one of the goals. The other player immediately acts as a defender and now a 1v1 game commences until a goal is scored or the ball leaves the pitch.

THOUGHTS

This practice asks many questions of both players. Can the player in possession use disguise in order to lose the defender and finish? Does the defender react quickly? Can the players show good skill, defending qualities, strength and composure to finish in a 1v1 situation?

SET-UP

⊛ Three groups of players, one group as left forwards, another as center forwards and the last group as right forwards.

⊛ The first player in the center forward line goes out and acts as the first target player.

⊛ On the coach's call a pass is played into the target player by the next middle forward. The target player has three choices:

1   Spin to the right and play a pass in behind the defender for the left forward to cross for him and the right forward.

2   Spin to the left and play a pass in behind the defender for the right forward to cross for him and the left forward.

3   Set middle passer who now plays a pass into one of the channels for the wide forward to cross.

THOUGHTS

This practice is set up to work on the target player's options in possession. The player has the freedom of choice on which teammate to pass to. All three teammates make supporting runs to receive and then react to the target player's pass.

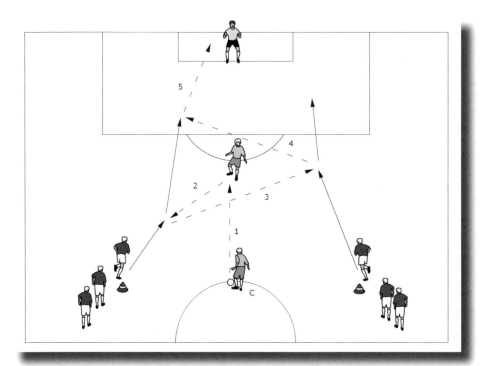

SET-UP

- ◉ Two groups of players, one keeper and two serving players/coaches as shown in the diagram.

- ◉ To start the practice, the first server passes long to the second server. Immediately one player from each line makes a supporting run to receive a set back. The server lays the balls off first time to his left or right. The player receiving quickly makes a one-two with the other supporting player and shoots at goal. The other player continues his run and looks for any rebounds.

THOUGHTS

This practice looks at the midfielders supporting a deep pass into the striker. The players are encouraged to use one touch and therefore the practice works quickly with four passes and a shot at goal. The second server has complete freedom on which player to set the ball to and therefore both supporting players must react accordingly. A simple progression to this practice is that the second server sets the ball back by using a throw with the supporting players using various techniques to complete a one-two.

SET-UP

⊙ 2 right footed players out on the right wing
  2 left footed players out on the left wing
  Groups of 2 players in the central area.

⊙ The coach passes to midfielder 1 who opens out and passes to midfielder 2 who then passes to the full back. The full back opens out and passes to the wide players. The wide player dribbles past the flag/cone and crosses for the two attackers.

⊙ The wide player has three movement choices; [1] away and to feet, [2] out and then inside and [3] to feet and then away into space behind.

⊙ Center midfielders become the next forwards.

PROGRESSION

⊙ The forwards pressure the centre midfielder before turning and attacking the cross.

⊙ The midfielders now attack the cross against the two forwards who have now become defenders.

THOUGHTS
Don't be predictable, any movement will cause a defender problems and give you both time and space in which to play. If you vary your movements your marker will struggle to read what is coming next.

SET-UP

⊛ One group of players and a keeper.

⊛ The group is split up as wide midfielders, center midfielders and center forwards as shown in the diagram.

⊛ To start the practice the wide player passes to the center midfielder who plays a return pass. The wide player then passes into the forward. The forward sets the supporting center midfielder who now has three choices;

  1. pass back into the path of the forward who has made a run to score
  2. pass wide for the wide midfielder who crosses for the forward to score
  3. switch play to the coach who crosses for the forward to score.

⊛ After the attack the wide player becomes a center midfielder, the center midfielder becomes a forward and the forward becomes a wide midfielder.

THOUGHTS

This session is set up to work on the center midfielder's supporting run and passing options. Do the same players always make the same choice? Is the timing of the support correct?

SET-UP

- One keeper, two teams as shown in the diagram.
- Each team send two players to act as the first crossers.
- To start the practice the coach calls out the color of the attacking team. The crosser for that team takes a touch out of his feet and crosses for his teammate to score. The first player on the other team acts as a defender and tries to stop him scoring. Once that ball has been scored or defended the roles reverse and now the other team's crosser takes a touch and crosses for his teammate to score.
- After each go the crossers jog back to the center and become attackers/defenders and the players who have just played have a turn at crossing.

THOUGHTS

The practice is designed to work on the attacker's movement to lose a defender and score from a cross. Can the attacker be clever in his movement? Can the defender react quickly and recover to defend well? Can the crosser pick out his teammate's run?

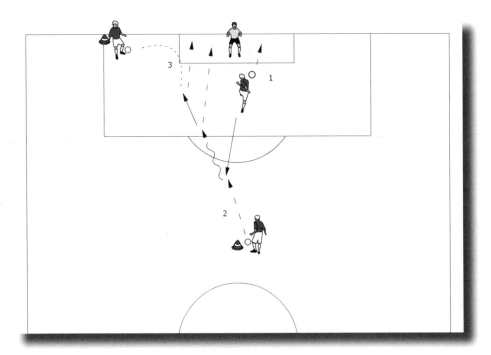

SET-UP

- One keeper, one active player, two servers as shown in the diagram.
- The active player has three different finishes inside the penalty box in quick succession.
- To start the practice the player takes a penalty against the keeper. He then immediately turns and receives a pass from the next player in line. He must turn and shoot first time, then receive a header from the second server.

THOUGHTS

This practice is a battle between the keeper and the active striker to see who is the King of the penalty area. The three quick shots are a test of the striker's all-round finishing abilities and the keeper's ability to recover to different types of finishing from various angles.

15   DRIBBLE, TAKE AND FINISH

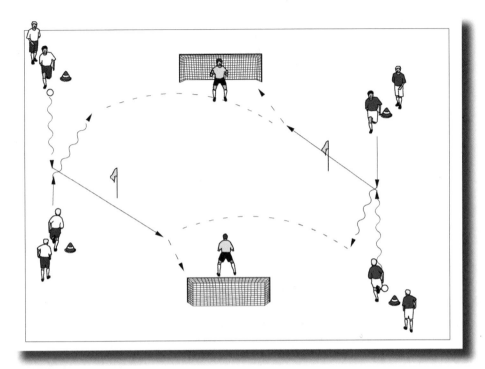

SET-UP

- Two lines of players and two keepers as shown in the diagram.
- The player in possession dribbles to meet his teammate. The teammate calls 'take', and then dribbles to cross. The original player now attacks the cross from the other wing.
- The players reverse roles for the next attack.

> **THOUGHTS**
> This practice has four players working and communicating at the same time, no players can switch off after their first movement as another action is required. The practice also requires that the players work at the same speed and intensity with good awareness of where and when to cross.

SET-UP

- One keeper, two servers, players working in pairs as shown in the diagram.

- One player acts as a forward and the other acts as defender. The attacker must lose his marker inside the small box by using quick movements and disguises.
  Once he leaves the box he must call the name of a server. The server then passes the ball to him for a shot.

- The players then become servers and reverse roles for their next turn as players.

THOUGHTS

This is a fun practice looking at ways in which to lose your marker. Also it looks at the defender's ability to recover and make a block or saving tackle.

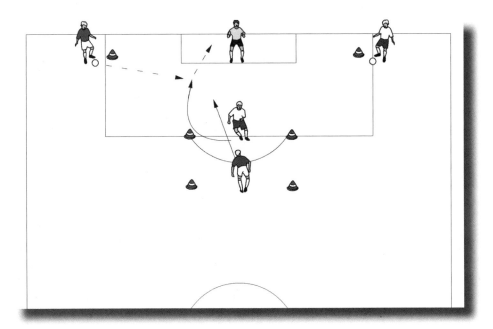

SET-UP

- The same set up as the previous practice as shown in the diagram
- This time the attacker starts nearer than the defender but faces away from the goal.
- The attacker must call the server, spin and hold off the defender to finish.

THOUGHTS

This time the defender has a slight advantage as he knows which server is going to pass and is facing his own goal. The attacker must use good disguise and movement before making his choice of server and use his body and strength to old off the defender and score.

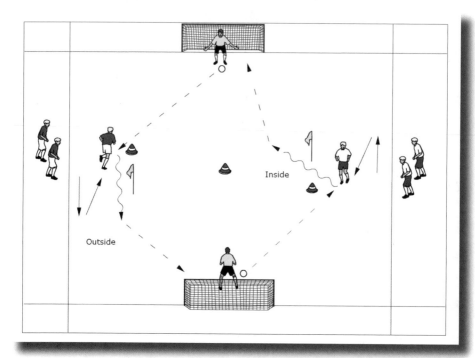

SET-UP

- ⊛ Two groups of players, two keepers and two servers/coaches as shown in the diagram.

- ⊛ The players move away and back to receive a pass from the keepers. The players then have two choices, they can either go outside or inside the flag/cone to shoot at goal.

THOUGHTS

This practice looks at the forward's movement to receive and his first touch giving him the opportunity to strike at goal. Encourage players to alternate going inside and outside the defender in order to add variation to their play and make it harder for the defenders to read their actions.

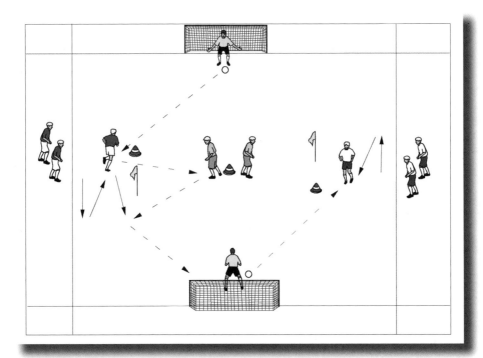

SET-UP

⊛ Same as previous practice as shown in the diagram.

⊛ This time the players have an added choice of playing a one-two with the server/ coach and receiving either inside or outside of the flag/cone.

THOUGHTS

This gives the players another picture in their minds. They still make good movements to receive but now with a teammate to use for a wall pass. Now the choices and options for the forward will make life extremely difficult for even the best defender.

SET-UP

⊛   Same as previous practice and as shown in the diagram.

⊛   The players make their own movements to receive but now play inside to the server/ coach, make an overlapping run across the front of the server and receive back for a shot.

THOUGHTS

This practice gives the players a fourth option when tightly marked around the penalty area. The player must pass first time to his teammate and move at top speed to overlap and lose his marker to finish.

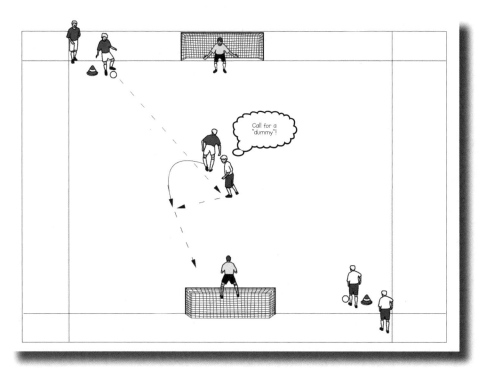

SET-UP

⊛ Two groups of players and two keepers as shown in the diagram.

⊛ A pass is played into the striker who dummies the ball, spins and receives a lay off to shoot.

⊛ The player who played the lay off spins and becomes the next shooter. The player who played the first pass now becomes the lay off player.

THOUGHTS

This practice is designed to work on the combination play and communication of the two forwards. Encourage the first forward to show good disguise in dummying the ball and to not always spin in the same direction. Also, the second striker must communicate with the first striker.

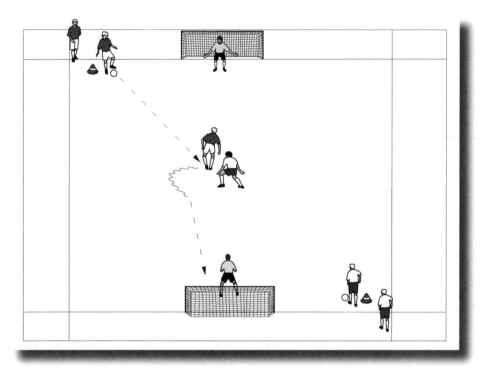

SET-UP

- The same set up as the previous practice and as shown in the diagram.
- This time the second player acts a 'passive defender'. The first striker receives a pass and must use a variation of realistic turns in order to lose the defender and shoot at goal.
- The passer follows his pass and becomes the defender for the next player. Therefore the roles are in this order; passer, defender, attacker and then rest.

THOUGHTS
This practice looks at the forward using good skill, disguise and strength in order to turn a tight marker and get a shot at goal. Encourage your players to show a variation of turns and to go both ways.

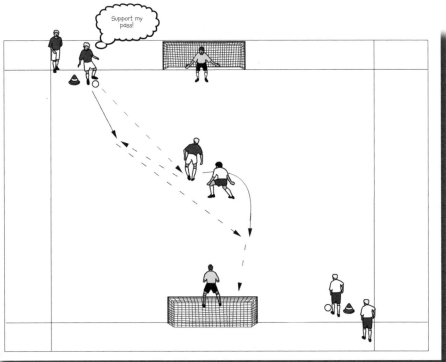

SET-UP

⊛ Same as previous practice and as shown in diagram.

⊛ This time the forward has the choice of turning the defender alone or setting the original passer and receiving a return pass in space to shoot.

⊛ The passer then becomes the defender for the next attack and then a forward.

THOUGHTS

This gives the forward another option if the defender does well and stops him turning. The forward must initially show good strength to hold up the ball and then show clever movement to receive the return pass. The simple progression to this practice is to play a normal 2v1 with the defender now defending for real.

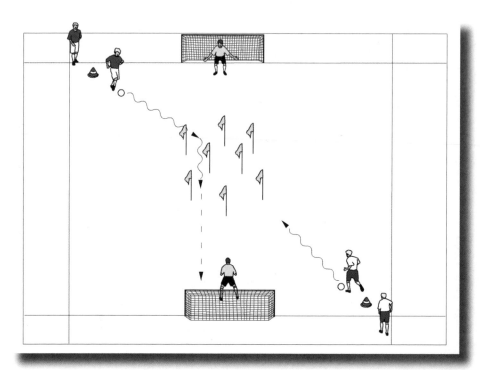

SET-UP

- Two keepers, two groups of players and a number of flag/poles as shown in the diagram.
- The players dribble into the crowd area, beat one or two mannequins/poles and then shoot at goal.
- Once the shot has been taken the players at the opposite end can start to dribble.

THOUGHTS

This practice is designed to look at what happens when forwards dribble into a crowded area or have defenders rushing out to block their shot. Can the forward beat one defender and then take a shot that avoids the defenders to score? The forward must use a variety of techniques such as placing, curling, bending and using power to score. The keeper is also worked in this practice as he will have his vision blocked by the mannequins/poles and the shot may also take a rebound which puts the keeper in a realistic game situation.

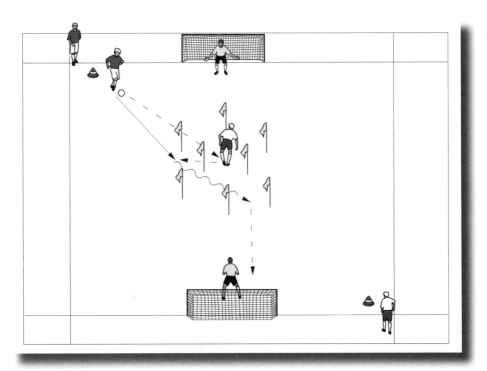

SET-UP

⊚ The same as in the previous practice and as shown in the diagram.

⊚ After taking a shot the player must remain in the middle of the crowded area and receive a pass from the player waiting to shoot. After making a pass the player then sprints into the crowded area, receives a lay off and now must take a good touch into space and clear of the mannequins/poles in order to shoot at goal.

> **THOUGHTS**
> Often in a match the ball comes to a player on the edge of the box and the quality of his first touch depends on whether he has the time and space to get a shot at goal. I have tried to recreate the situation in this practice where the player's first touch must take him away from the defender to give him an opportunity to score.

SET-UP

- A number of players spread out around the five stations and a goalkeeper as shown in the diagram.
- Players move to the next station on their left after each go.
- To start the practice the keeper throws the ball out to player number 1, who has one touch to control and shoot. Immediately after the shot, a diagonal ball is played to player number 2 who must shoot first time. After this shot a diagonal ball is played to player number 3 who now has a 1v1 with the passing player acting as a defender.

THOUGHTS

This session is a competition for the players to see how many goals they can score in a set time. The practice runs very quickly and gives the players lots of opportunities to shoot and work on different techniques in order to score.

SET-UP

⊛ A number of players spread out on the four stations and goalkeeper in the goal.

⊛ Each time the player is at station one, he acts as the defender

⊛ To start the practice, the defender comes out to the middle and receives a serve from player A. The defender must make a headed clearance out of the box.
Immediately player B dribbles down the side and crosses for player A to lose the defender and score. Once this ball leaves play, player C dribbles into the area and plays 1v1 against the defender.

⊛ All players move to the station on their left after each go.

THOUGHTS

This is a fun finishing practice that also works on a defender's role. The players like this prac-tice as the defender tries to beat the attackers by defending well and getting a point for each ball he defends well. He gets one point for heading out of the area without the ball bouncing, another point for successfully clearing the cross and another point for defending well in a 1v1 situation. The attackers must try their best to get points by scoring goals.

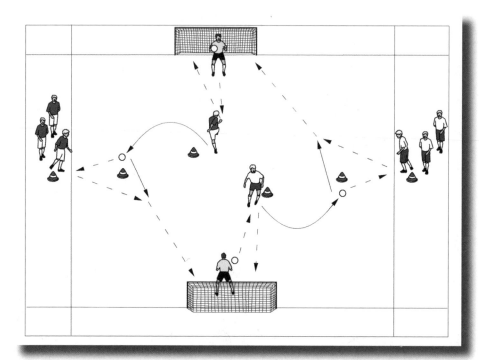

SET-UP

- ⊛ Two groups of players and two keepers as shown in the diagram.
- ⊛ To start the practice the keepers throw a ball to the forwards who must volley first time to score. Immediately the forwards spin and play a one-two to finish in the other goal.

THOUGHTS

This practice again works on various techniques to score in quick succession. The players have to adjust to the serve from the keeper and finish first time, then they must react at speed to play a one-two. Variations/progressions to the session can be made simply by the keeper now throwing for a header and the forward now doing a skill and then dribbling past the manne-quins/cone to shoot.

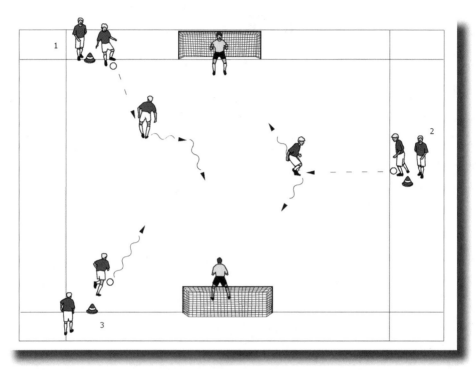

SET-UP

⊛ Two keepers and three groups of players as shown in the diagram.

⊛ Station one goes first, then station two and then station three.

⊛ At station one the defender passes to the attacker who must turn and dribble to score. The defender tries to recover and stop the attacker scoring. At station two the defender passes to the attacker who must use disguise to turn and attack one of the goals while the defender tries to recover and stop him scoring. At station three the attacker has three touches to score in a 1v1 with the keeper.

⊛ After 3-5 minutes the groups rotate and play the next role.

THOUGHTS
This practice forces the attacker to play at speed and under real game pressure. The attacker's speed of thought and strength will be a key to whether he is successful in scoring a goal.

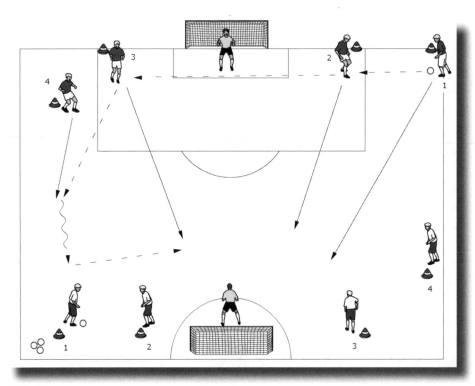

SET-UP

- ⊛ Two keepers and groups of four players as shown in the diagram.

- ⊛ Player 1 passes to player 2 who runs and passes to player 3. Player 3 then passes down the wing for player 4 to run and cross for players 1, 2 and 3 to finish.

- ⊛ The players rotate positions in the line up, wait for their turn and then attack the opposite goal.

THOUGHTS

The practice is set up to work on the team build-up play to finish. Variations can be used. Instead of player 2 passing to player 3, he could pass directly to player 4 who dribbles inside and plays a reverse pass to an overlapping player 3.

Players must ensure that they time their runs and don't get into the box too early; also they must not be in front of the crosser and therefore be in an offside position.

31 ■ WIDE PLAYER GOES INSIDE OR OUTSIDE TO CROSS

SET-UP

- ⊛ Two groups of four players, one group acting as crossers, the other group acting as forwards and one keeper in goal.
- ⊛ The resting crosser passes to the working crosser and then pressures him as a full back. The crosser must beat the defender down the line or by cutting inside to cross for the forwards.
- ⊛ The forwards must make a crossover run and vary their movements into the box.
- ⊛ After a set time, the forwards and crossers rotate.

THOUGHTS

Wide players that can cross well with both feet are a must in the modern game. For a defender it is a real headache as coaches often tell their full backs to force wide players onto their weaker side. If from a young age players are comfortable crossing from both feet and accustomed to going inside and outside defenders they will be hard to stop in game situations.

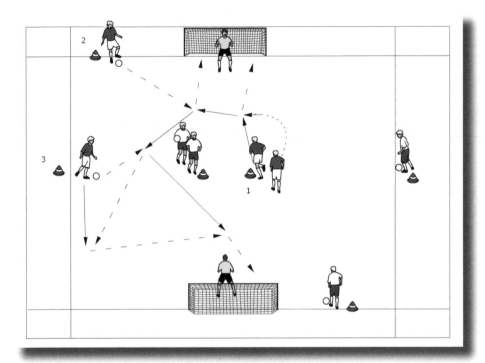

SET-UP

⊚ 3 groups of players and two keepers.

⊚ Two groups work while one group act as servers.

⊚ To start the practice the second player in line throws a ball over the attackers head, the attacker must react and use a half-volley technique to shoot, immediately the attacker receives a thrown pass from server 2 and he must volley or head to score, then they spin and plays a one-two with server 3 who crosses for him to finish at the other end.

⊚ After a set time, all the teams rotate and have a turn as the servers.

> **THOUGHTS**
> This practice gives the attacker a series of different serves and problems to deal with in order to score. Can the player constantly adjust to the different serves and still show good technique and accuracy in finishing? The two working attackers are in a competition to see who can score the most goals and finish the three attacks the quickest.

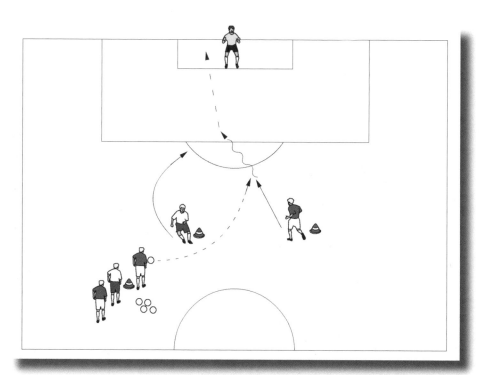

SET-UP

- ◉ One keeper and a number of players as shown in the diagram.
- ◉ The first player in line goes to the third cone and acts as the forward. The second player goes to the second cone and faces away from the goal as the defender. The third player starts on the first cone and acts as the server. After each go the players move up a cone.
- ◉ The server throws the ball in the air, past the defender and in the direction of the forward. The forward must run and control the ball out of the air and hold off the recovering defender in order to score.

THOUGHTS
This practice looks at the forward's first touch and strength when under pressure from a recovering defender. Does the forward take a first touch across the defender's running path or does he use his arms and strength to hold off the defender in order to shoot?

SET-UP

- One keeper, three groups of players as shown in the diagram.
- The central player makes a pass to either side of the defender and into the path of either the player to his right or left. The defender turns and tries to recover while the forward tries to dribble and score.
- After each turn the passer becomes a defender, the defender joins the line from which the attacker left and the attacker becomes the passer.

THOUGHTS

This practice looks at how a forward finishes under pressure from a recovering defender. Can the forward hold the defender off? Does he decide to cut across the defender's running path?

CONTROLLING THE BALL OUT OF THE AIR TO SCORE

SET-UP

⊛ One keeper, three groups of players. Two groups working, one group acting as servers.

⊛ After each shot the player moves to the next station to his left.

⊛ After a set time, the teams rotate and all have the chance to rest as servers.

⊛ **Station 1**; the server throws the ball to the player and adds 'passive' pressure, the attacker must touch to one side and finish with his next touch. **Station 2**; the server throws to the attacker who controls to the floor, dribbles in and out of the mannequins/cones and shoots. **Station 3**; the server throws over the attacker's head who must control before the ball hits the ground and then dribbles to shoot.

> **THOUGHTS**
> This practice looks at the attacker's first touch when dealing with a ball out of the air. Can he get the ball under control quickly in order to get the chance to score?

SET-UP

- 4 sessions in one format
- Session 1   A   Dribbles and shoots,

  B   Passes and receives a lay off from A and shoots,

  C   Plays 2v1 with A against player B.

- Session 2   A   Dribbles and shoots,

  B   Plays 1v1 with player A,

  C   Choice; calls out the name of a teammate he wants and plays 2v1 against each other.

- Session 3   A   Dribbles and shoots,

  B   Passes to player B, receives a lay off then passes wide for player C,

  C   Crosses for players A and B to finish

- Session 4   A   Dribbles and shoots,

  B   Passes to player A, receives a return pass then passes wide to player C

  C   Crosses for player B who loses player A [defender] and tries to score.

SET-UP

- One keeper and a squad of players spread out over the five stations as shown in the diagram.
- The players move on to the next station after each go.
- The practice starts at station 1, a one-two is played with the player at station 2 and then a through ball is played for player 3 to shoot at goal. Immediately after the shot, the player at station 4 dribbles and beats the flag/cone on the inside or down the line and crosses to the player at station 5 who shoots at goal.
- The process continues for a set period.

THOUGHTS

This session looks at the roles of the attacking central and wide midfielders and encourages them to get in the box and have a strike at goal. The shooter at station 3 is a central midfielder breaking past the striker in order to get a chance of scoring while the player at station 5 is a wide midfielder who is attacking a cross from the opposite side of the pitch.

SET-UP

- One keeper, groups of three players as shown in the diagram.
- The center midfielder plays a pass out to the wide player who passes to the forward; the center midfielder makes a run to support. The forward now has four choices in possession:

  1 set the wide midfielder who plays the center midfielder through on goal to shoot,
  2 play down the line for the wide player to cross to the center forward,
  3 turn down the line and cross for the center forward,
  4 turn inside and play the center midfielder through.

- The players should rotate the midfielder each time.
- A simple progression is that the wide player now has the choice as they dictate what the forward does by communicating after their pass. 'Set' would be choice 1, 'One-two' would be choice 2, 'Turn' would be choice 3 and 'Time' would be choice 4.

THOUGHTS

This practice looks at the midfielders having the ability and confidence to get past their forwards and score a goal. Goal scoring midfielders are invaluable to any team at any level and this practice gives them four situations that occur in real games.

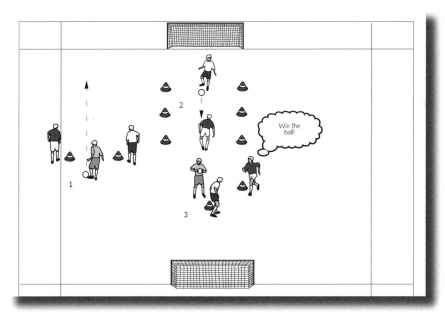

SET-UP

- Three areas as shown in the diagram, players in groups of two. Keepers can be used if available.
- **Area 1**, the coach passes the ball down towards the by-line. The attacker and defender chase after the ball. The attacker tries to cross the ball in order to get a point while the defender gets points if he manages to stop him.
- **Area 2**, the defender passes to the attacker who must have at least one touch before trying to score. If the attacker manages to get a shot on target he gets the point, if the defender stops him by blocking the shot or forcing him out of the area then he gets the point.
- **Area 3**, the coach throws the ball over the defender's head for the attacker to run onto, the attacker gets the point if he manages to put the ball into the goal while the defender gets the point for getting to the ball first and clearing.

THOUGHTS

This circuit works on small but vital situations that occur in every game. The players must work on these defending areas which are hard to coach. I have found that this circuit enables you to work on these areas but is also challenging and fun for the players as they compete against each other to get the most points. Ensure that each player does a circuit as the attacker and then the defender.

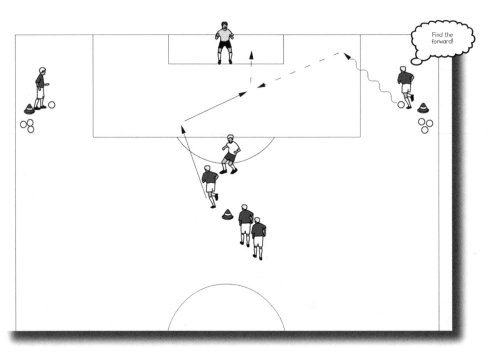

SET-UP

⊛   Two wide players, one keeper and a group of players working as attackers/defenders.

⊛   To start the practice the wide player dribbles diagonally towards the by-line and looks to cut the ball back for the center forward who loses his marker and scores with a first time finish.

⊛   After being a forward you then become a defender before resting.

THOUGHTS

This practice looks at the movement choices of the center forward when trying to receive a cut back to score. The defender will obviously have to pay attention to the ball and the players so it will be difficult to defend against quick movement. I give my forwards three movement options;

     1   Away to the far post then quickly get across the defender to the near post.

     2   Towards the near and then away to receive between the defender and keeper at the far post.

     3   Run quickly to take the defender towards the goal before holding your run to receive to feet.

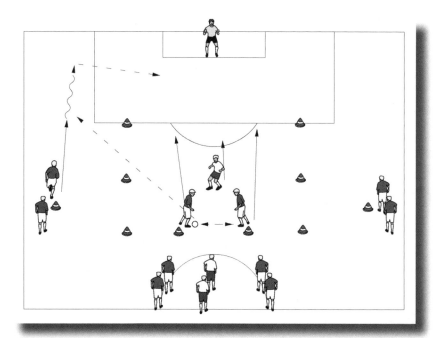

SET-UP

⊛ Two left sided players

⊛ Two right sided players

⊛ Groups of three in the middle [one acts as a defender]

⊛ The two attacking players in the middle pass the ball to each other. When they are ready and with disguise they play the ball down one of the flanks for the wide player to run after and cross. The two central attackers try to lose the defender and score.

PROGRESSION

⊛ The resting wide player starts 10 yards behind the wide player who is going to cross and chases back so that the wide player has to play at a 'real game' pace.

THOUGHTS

The practice is designed to work on the movement of two attackers to lose a defender in the box as well as the wide player's ability to pick out the free attacker whether at the near or far post. The attacker's movement and success is usually poor to start but with a few attempts he will be trying different crossovers and fakes in order to gain that vital extra inch of space to score.

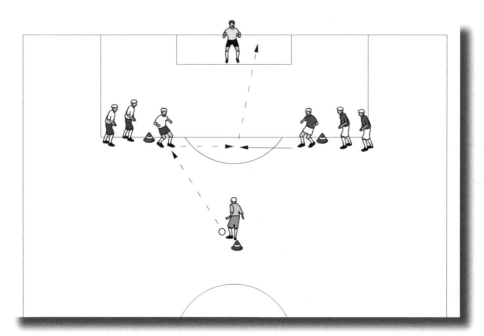

SET-UP

- One keeper, two lines of players as shown in the diagram
- The coach passes to one of the teams who plays a first time pass across to the other team. The first player on the other team meets the pass and finishes. The first passer goes in for rebounds. The different types of service and finishes used can vary , for example;
  - Control with inside right, finish left
  - Control with inside left, finish right
  - First time right
  - First time left
  - Thrown serve, volley pass and finish first time
  - Thrown serve, headed pass and finish first time

THOUGHTS

This practice looks at quick combination and finishing around the box. The players have to combine quickly in order to get a shot at goal and follow up for any rebounds. In a game you only have a split second to get a shot on goal before defenders try to pressure. The varying of service and types of lay off enables players to react to different situations.

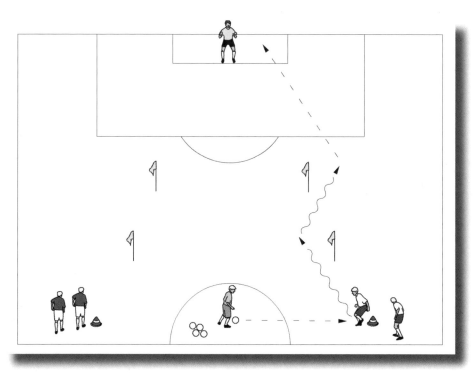

SET-UP

- Two groups of players and a keeper
- The coach passes to the player on his right. The player can either go inside then outside of the defender or outside and then inside in order to shoot at goal. Ideally the players will only take three touches before shooting. One touch inside, second touch outside, then the shot.
- Once the player shoots, the coach passes to the player on the left. Shooting players retrieve their ball and join the opposite line.

THOUGHTS

This practice looks at beating two defenders at pace on the inside and outside before finishing. This type of strong, quick and direct play is hard for the defenders as the attacking player doesn't give them time to adjust and make a tackle. The attacking player should try to have as few touches as possible before shooting.

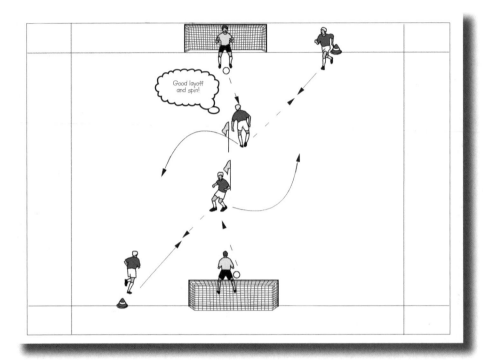

SET-UP

- Two keepers and two groups of players as shown in the diagram.
- Both keepers start with the ball and roll out to the forward who sets his supporting teammate, spins and receives a pass in order to shoot at the opposite goal.
- The supporting player now becomes the next forward/shooter.
- The keepers can vary their serve so that the forward has to use various areas of his body in order to set the supporting player [pass, chest, head, volley etc]

THOUGHTS

This practice works on the forward's first touch and ability to lay off to the supporting mid-fielder before making an arcing run into space to finish. The arc of the forward's run and the weight of the supporting player's through pass are crucial to the practice as either can affect the chance of getting a good shooting opportunity.

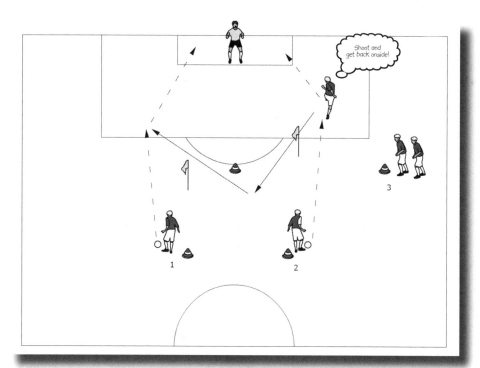

SET-UP

- ◉ This practice has one keeper and a group of players spread out across the three stations.
- ◉ The player at station 2 passes into the forward who has pulled off the defender/flag in order to have a touch and a shot at goal.. Immediately, the forward reacts and gets back onside before darting back inside the other defender/flag in order to receive a pass from station 1.
- ◉ Players start at station 1, before moving to station 2 and then as the shooter at station 3.

THOUGHTS

This practice has two key working areas, one is to work on the forward's quick movements and reactions around the box and the other is to use the new outlook on the offside laws which state a player isn't offside if he quickly gets back onside before moving forward again. The forward in this practice must visualize the opportunity available if he can quickly get back into an onside position. This type of run back onside and then into space is very difficult for defenders who are usually caught watching the ball.

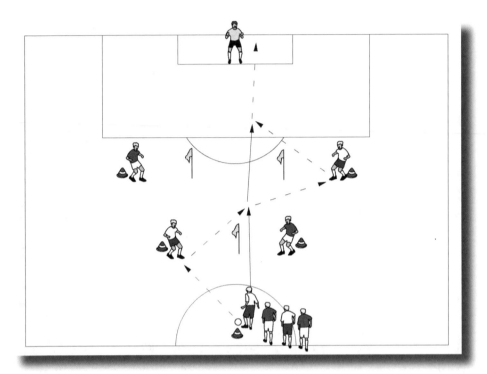

SET-UP

- ⊛ Two groups of four players and a keeper. Each team has two players working and two players resting/setters.

- ⊛ The first player starts with a ball, dribbles and plays a one-two with his teammate.; He then has one touch and then plays another one-two with his other teammate before having a first time shot.

- ⊛ The players should rotate between setters and shooters after a set time.

THOUGHTS

This practice was designed for midfielders who constantly try to run with the ball through tight areas. The practice aims to show them that a quick give and go combination can break through these areas and give you a chance to score. The players should be encouraged to have as few touches as possible and pass with both feet as they make their way to goal.

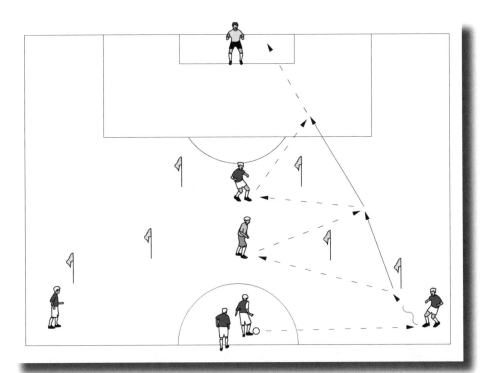

SET-UP

- ⊛ One keeper, group of players on the half-way line. One player comes out as a left mid, one as a right mid and one as a forward.
- ⊛ The passer plays wide to the right midfielder who dribbles inside. The pass into the striker is now blocked but the player still has three options;

  1   Beat the next player before playing a one-two with the forward and shooting.
  2   Pass inside to the center mid [coach] who plays to the forward who returns to the wide player in the box.
  3   Play a one-two with the center mid [coach] and the center forward in order to shoot [shown in diagram].

THOUGHTS

This practice helps to show the wide players their options when forced to play inside by their marker. The wide player's first priority is to play forward to the striker but that isn't always possible, so the practice looks at the next available options open to the player.

SET-UP

- Two keepers and two groups of players as shown in the diagram
- The player acting as the first defender starts in the 10x10 yd area. The first dribbler tries to get past and through to the other side. If he manages to get through success fully another player attempts to dribble across. The defender must try to win the ball and then is free to dribble and try to score against the keeper. The player who lost the ball is now the defender and the game continues.
- The defender who stays in the area for the longest number of goes is the loser.

THOUGHTS

This is a fun way to work on both 1v1 dribbling and defending. The dribbling player knows he must do his best to avoid being tackled or forced too wide while the defender knows that if he defends well he will have a chance to attack and score.

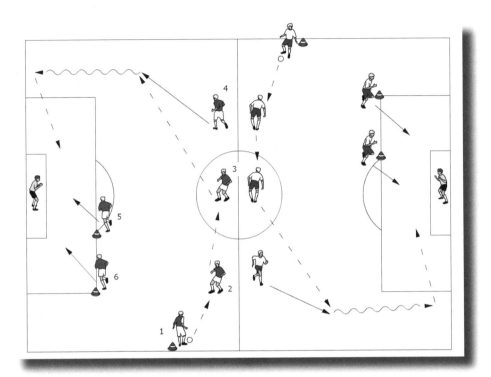

SET-UP

⊛ The practice is set up as shown in the diagram and has six distinct roles: left mid, ` right mid, center mid, near post run and far post run.

⊛ The resting player passes to the left mid who opens and passes to the center mid. The center mid opens and dribbles before passing to the right mid, who has got wide by the touchline. The right midfielder dribbles and crosses for the near post and far post runners to score.

⊛ Players move from roles 1 to 6 before resting.

THOUGHTS

This practice looks at how the team opens up from one side of the pitch to the other. Initially the right midfielder is tucked in as the team are attacking down the left side but as the pass is played inside to the center midfielder, the player has to get himself out wide in order to receive a pass in space to dribble and cross.

Good touch and strike!

SET-UP

⊕ Three stations with players spread evenly amongst them and one keeper as shown in the diagram.

⊕ The first player passes down to the second who sets first time. The first player now plays a diagonal pass to the third player who touches out of his feet and shoots at goal.

THOUGHTS
A practice looking at the timing, weight and speed of pass in a combination of one touch passes to shoot.

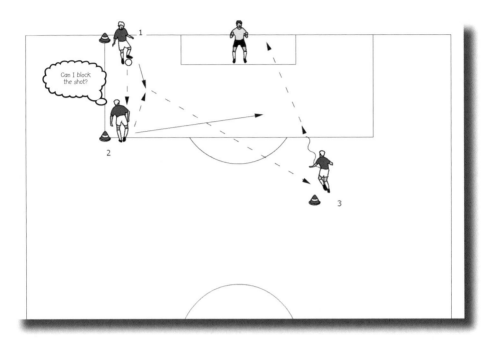

SET-UP

⊛   Three stations with players spread evenly amongst them and one keeper as shown in the diagram.

⊛   The player 1 passes to player 2 who returns first time. The first player then plays a diagonal pass to player 3 to touch and finish. Once player 2 lays the pass off he becomes a defender and pressures player 3.

THOUGHTS
This practice progresses from the previous one and now ensures that the passing tempo and weight must be accurate in order for player 3 to shoot, otherwise the defender will get a block on the shot and stop the attack.

SET-UP

- Three stations with players spread evenly amongst them and one keeper as shown in the diagram.

- This time the practice involves five one-touch passes and a shot. Player 1 passes to player 2 who sets and spins. Player 1 then plays a diagonal pass to player 3 who plays a one-two with the supporting player 2 and shoots.

THOUGHTS

This progression adds to the passing and the intensity with all passes having to be accurate in order for player 3 to get a shot at goal.

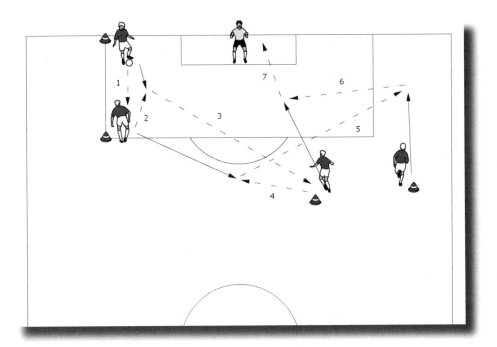

SET-UP

⊙ Four stations with players spread evenly amongst them and one keeper as shown in the diagram.

⊙ This time the practice involves six passes and one shot. Player 1 passes to player 2 who sets and spins. Player 1 then passes to player 3 who sets to the supporting player 2. Player 2 plays out wide for player 4 who crosses first time for player 3 to finish.

THOUGHTS

This progression advances by adding a wide player to the set up. The build up now has six one-touch passes before a goal and it is essential that all players are ready to receive and use the correct weight and type of pass in order to get a cross and finish.

SET-UP

- Two groups of players and a keeper, set up as shown in the diagram.
- The first player comes out and receives a pass from the opposite group, opens out and dribbles at the center flag/pole. He beats the "defender" to the left or right and has a shot at goal, trying to avoid the other mannequins/poles.
- The player that passed now has to go as the shooter and receives a pass from the opposite line.

THOUGHTS

This practice looks at beating a defender and getting a good shot off from outside the box. The player must keep the ball close as he beats the first defenders or he could be tackled or have his shot blocked by the other defenders.

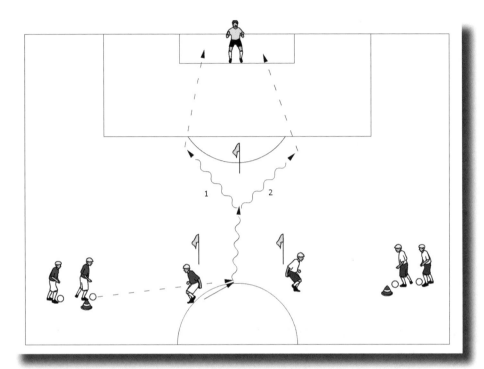

SET-UP

- One keeper, two groups of players as shown in the diagram.
- The first player from both groups comes out and receives a pass from their line. The player lets the ball run across his body and past the first defender. Then the player dribbles at the next defender before beating him to the left or right and shooting from outside the box.

> **THOUGHTS**
> This practice looks at the space that can be created by receiving the ball side on and letting it run across your body and past a defender. The player must show disguise in letting the ball run across the body and then accelerate away into the space created in order to beat the next defender and shoot.

SET-UP

- Three groups of players and a keeper, set up as shown in the diagram.

- The defender dribbles and then passes to the first attacker, the attacker dribbles at the defender who now jockeys. When the players reach the cone the defender forces the attacker to turn and now the defender forces them backwards. The attacker then passes across the box for his teammate to shoot. The defender must now react and get across in order to tackle the attacker or block the shot on goal.

THOUGHTS

This practice looks at different types of defending in and around the box. This type of defending is not often fun for players but I have found they enjoy this game due to the competition of trying not to concede a goal.

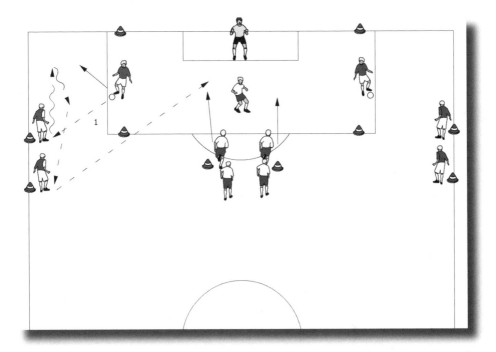

SET-UP

⊛ Three groups of four players and a keeper as shown in the diagram. One group of players act as wide players and full backs, one group act as defenders and one group act as forwards.

⊛ To start, the defending full back passes to the wide player. The wide player tries to beat the defender down the line and cross and turn back and set his full back for a first time cross towards the two attackers in the box.

⊛ The players rotate roles. The defenders have a go as a left full back, center back, right full back and then rest a turn. The attackers just work in pairs while the wide players and attacking full backs take one turn at each of the different roles. The team rotate after a set time.

THOUGHTS

The practice is designed to look at the wide players' ability to beat their full back and get a cross into the box and also to teach the wide player that if its not on, then turn back to a supporting full back who can cross. The attackers must always be on the move and constantly making different runs.

SET-UP

- One keeper, group of players on the half-way line, one player goes right midfield, one goes left midfield and one starts as a forward.
- To start the practice the first player passes out to the left midfielder who dribbles inside and plays a pass inside the center back/flag for the forward who has bent his run in order to stay onside and finish.
- After passing you follow and become a wide player, after a wide player you become the forward. The next attack comes from the other side.

THOUGHTS

This practice looks at what happens when a wide player has been forced inside. The forward has two options; either call and receive to feet or bend the run and receive the ball into space. This practice focuses on the striker bending his run and getting in on the blind side of the central defender. This is very hard to defend against if the wide player is quick and accurate with his pass and the forward has made the correct run.

SET-UP

- To start, the drill needs two full backs, two center backs, two center midfielders and two center forwards. Other players wait and become full backs after the first attack.
- Both goalkeepers start the practice by throwing out to their full backs. The four players combine to end up with a cross and a shot at goal. The coach should give the players three to four different variations. An example of a move would be:

> Goalkeeper to full back, full back to center forward, forward sets center mid fielder, center midfielder passes down the line for wide player, who crosses for the center forward to finish.

The players should have complete freedom on which variation they choose and should make realistic game movements to receive each pass. After the first attack all players shift up a position. Full backs to center midfield, then to a wide player and then to a forward before starting as a full back going the other way.

THOUGHTS

This practice works on the players' passing options during the game and gives them pictures in their minds so that when a ball is in a certain position they know exactly what movement to make and which pass to play. Repetition in training enhances all the players' understanding and enables the group to play quick and decisive football.

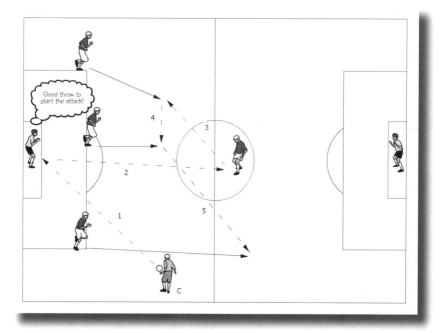

SET-UP

- Players work in groups of four and line up as a midfield three with one attacker. After each attack the players should switch roles.
- The coach plays a ball into the goalkeeper to start. The keeper throws long to the center forward who sets the ball back to one of the supporting wide players. The wide player plays inside to the center midfielder who switches play to the furthest wide player. The wide player receives and dribbles down the wing to cross for the other players to finish.
- The players are not told how many touches to have initially but the coach can add fun to the session and competition between groups of players by timing how long it takes to attack from one end to the other.

THOUGHTS

The practice is used to create fast counter attacking football in which the players both support and pass at real match speed and with quick decisions. This style of attacking play at high speed is almost unstoppable if the players are aware of each other and don't slow down the build-up by having too many touches.

SET-UP

- Groups of four players, three act as attackers and one as a defender as shown in the diagram.
- The three attackers come in close together as if to stop a pass through them by the defender. The defender then makes a poor pass straight to the left attacker.
  The left attacker passes across to the center attacker who then dribbles and passes out to the right attacker who is now wide and free to dribble and cross. The left attacker and the attacker get into the box and try to lose the defender and score.
- After being a crosser you become the defender, after defender then left attacker and then the center attacker so that every player plays all the roles in the practice.

THOUGHTS

This practice looks at how the team opens up from winning possession in the center of the pitch. The team must start with a good defensive shape with both wide players tucked in, to stop any passes directly through the center of the team. On winning possession the players must open out and make the pitch as big as possible, then play across midfield, out wide and finally down the wing for a cross.

SET-UP

- One keeper, two groups of four players. One group act as supporting attackers while one group split up into four positions, center mid, target forward, wide left and wide right.

- To start, the center mid passes into the target player who sets one of the supporting players. The receiving supporting player plays a square pass to their teammate who then plays down the line for one of the wide players; both supporting players get into the box for the cross and try to score.

- Rotate the teams after a set time.

THOUGHTS

This practice looks at two center midfielders supporting a forward pass from the defense into the central target forward, then combining before attacking the box to finish. After a few attempts you may point out to the midfielders that in a real game you don't want both players to attack the box and therefore one should hold back on the edge for any knockdowns or rebounded shots.

63 ▰▰▰ MIDFIELD SUPPORT OF TARGET MAN (PROGRESSION)

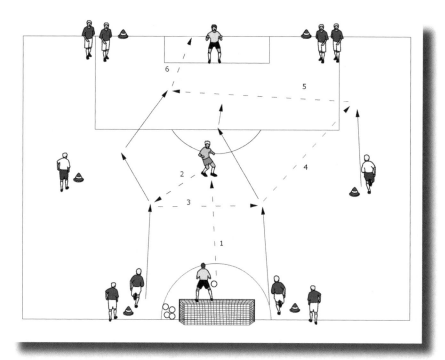

SET-UP

⊛ A group of players at each end working in pairs, two keepers and two crossers as shown in the diagram.

⊛ The keeper starts the practice by throwing the ball into the target player who sets one of the two supporting midfielders. The receiving midfielder plays a pass across to his teammate who then plays down the line for the wide player to cross for both midfielders who have continued their runs into the box. The next attack comes from the opposite end.

PROGRESSION 2

⊛ One defender is placed in each penalty box and two midfielders now have to lose their defender in order to convert the cross from the wide player.

THOUGHTS

This practice looks at the supporting play of midfielders to a forward pass. Can they combine in order to get the ball wide and can one or both players get into the box and score from the cross? Goal scoring midfielders are essential to any team and this practice helps develop this type of player.

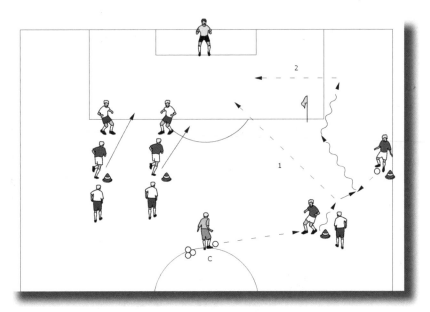

SET-UP

- ○ A keeper and two groups of players working in pairs. Each team has one wide player out on the wing as shown in the diagram.

- ○ The first wide player receives a pass from coach 1, and as he is under no initial pressure they cross early in the box for their two forwards, immediately he reacts and runs to receive another pass from coach 2, this time the flag is close and acts as a pressuring defender. The wide player must now beat the flag/pole on the outside and cross from the by-line for the two forwards.

- ○ Each time the forwards attack two crosses and then act as defenders for two crosses. The coach keeps the score between the two teams and this adds a real game competitive edge.

THOUGHTS

Although this practice has coaching areas for both the attackers and defenders in terms of movements and areas to attack/defend, this practice is all about developing the awareness and skill of wide players. In order to be unpredictable to their marker a wide player must mix up his game between dribbling inside, passing quickly, crossing early or beating his opponent down the line. This practice helps the players with these decisions and shows them that if the opponent sits off, then don't give up the opportunity to cross quickly from deep areas. However, if they get tight then use the space in behind by beating him with pace and crossing from the by-line.

SET-UP

- ⊛ One keeper, a group of players and three mannequins/poles to act as defenders
- ⊛ To start, both attackers make an angled run off the mannequins to receive. The central player makes a pass to the player of his choice. The receiving attacker turns quickly while the attacker not receiving reacts and makes a run in behind the defenders in order to receive a pass and then get a shot at goal.
- ⊛ The player that gets the chance to shoot is replaced by the player who started the practice.

> **THOUGHTS**
> This practice looks at the movement of two strikers in order to receive a pass from their midfielders, and how they react to the first pass in order to move again and combine to score a goal. This practice was designed after watching the Chelsea FC and Argentina forward Hernan Crespo closely. Crespo is constantly on the move in order to receive a pass or lose a defender and is a real inspiration to watch for any young forward with dreams of becoming a top player.

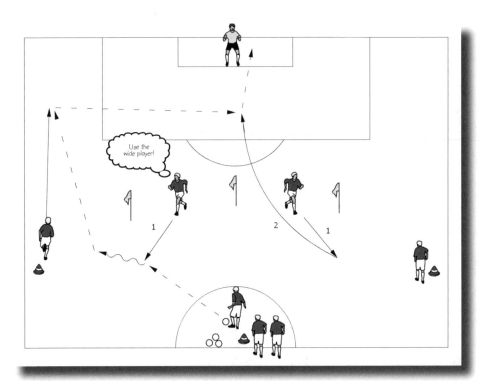

SET-UP

- One keeper, two wide players and a group of players acting a forwards.
- To start, both forwards make an angled run off the defenders in order to receive a pass. The midfielder passes to the forward of his choice. The forward receiving turns out and plays a ball down the line to his wide player. The other forward reacts and makes a second run in order to score from the cross.
- For the next attack the midfielder takes the place of the forward who has attacked the cross.

THOUGHTS

This practice progresses from the previous one with the addition of two wide players. The forward now has the option of turning outside and passing down the line or turning inside and playing his forward partner through on goal. The forward not receiving must now be aware and ready to react to his strike partner's movement and choice.

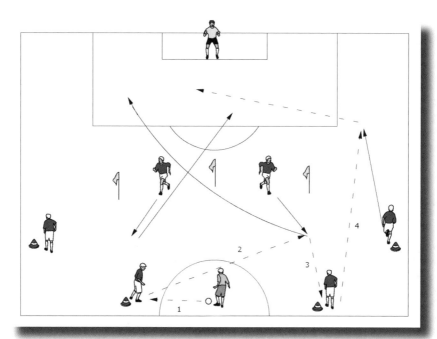

SET-UP

- One keeper, two wide players and a group of players acting as midfielders/forwards
- To start, the coach passes to his left or right. The forward opposite the midfielder receiving makes a run off the defenders in order to receive a diagonal pass.
  On receiving, the forward sets the other midfielder who makes a pass down the line for the wide player.
  The forward who came short makes a run to the far post while the other forward makes a run across the defense and into the near post area in order to score from the cross.
- For the next attack the two midfielders become the forwards.

> **THOUGHTS**
> This practice looks at how effective a second/loose striker can be in a team's build-up. The defender will have to weigh the options of going with the striker and leaving space in behind for the other striker to receive a pass into or holding his position and allowing the attacker to receive. This creates confusion in the defense and enables the team to play forward into dangerous attacking areas. Examples of this type of player are Ronaldinho, Del Piero, Totti, and Rooney.

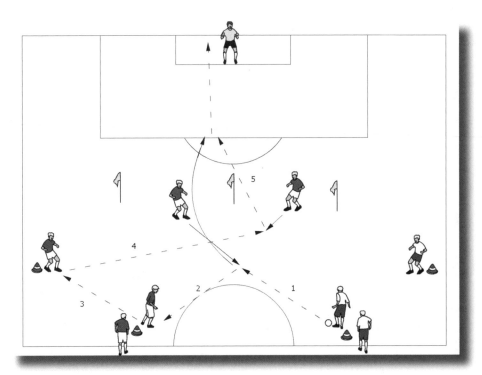

SET-UP

- One keeper, two groups of four players,

- To start, the midfielder passes diagonally into the forward who has come short to receive. The forward turns and plays to the other midfielder who then passes out wide. The wide player then comes inside and plays into the target forward. The original forward now makes a forward run in behind the defense in order to receive a through pass from the target forward.

- The players all move up a position on their side of the pitch, therefore the left center midfielder becomes the left wide player and the left wide player becomes the center forward. The next attack starts from the opposite side.

THOUGHTS

This is a progression from the previous practice and now looks at when the defender follows the forward when he goes to receive the ball. The forward must now set the ball back and then wait to make a well timed run and receive a pass from his forward partner into space behind the defense.

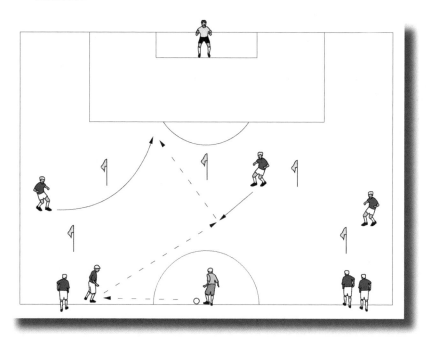

SET-UP

- One keeper, three groups of players: left full back/wide players, right full back/wide players and center midfielders/forwards

- The center midfielder starts the practice by passing out to one of the full backs. The full back looks to play wide but the defender/flag is stopping a pass into the wide player, therefore the full back plays a diagonal pass into the center forward who has come off his marker to receive. Immediately the wide player makes a run off the line and in-between the opposition's full back and center back in order to receive a through pass from the forward.

- The full back becomes a wide player and the midfielder becomes a forward for the next attack.

> **THOUGHTS**
> This practice was designed to encourage the wide players to make runs off the line which are both hard to defend and also create confusion in defenses over who is going to pick up the run. I was inspired to work on this type of movement by the style of players like Freddie Ljungberg, Arjen Robben and Damien Duff who regularly make this run to score and create goals in the English Premier League.

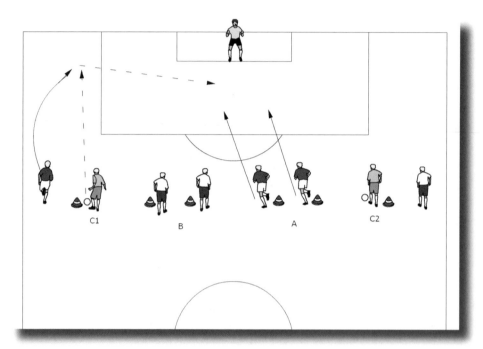

SET-UP

⊛ Two coaches, one keeper, and ten players as shown in the diagram. The coaches can be exchanged for two extra crosses if you have the right amount of players available.

⊛ To start, coach number one passes down the line for the first wide player to run and drive a low, hard cross into the box between the six yard area and the penalty spot. Two forwards from the furthest group attack the cross with one group to the near post and one attacking the far post.

⊛ The next attack comes from the other side.

THOUGHTS

This session was designed down to a personal preference for low, hard crosses into the box. I feel that this type of cross, especially in youth soccer, provides the best chance of scoring as often just a touch from an attacker or defender can see the ball fly into the net. If the wide player can cross the ball between the six yard line and penalty spot this type of cross is even more difficult to defend as a keeper will find it very difficult to come and pick up and could cause even more uncertainty between the keeper and defenders.

SET-UP

- Two keepers and two groups of 6 players in a 15x15 yard area.
- The players on each team are numbered 1 to 6. The first player on each team goes into the middle of the area. The player must make 4 quick one-twos with his teammates before dribbling out of the area for a 1v1 with the keeper.
- Each team should always have four players on the outside, one in the middle working and a player getting back from his shot.

THOUGHTS

This practice is designed to teach midfield players that by passing quickly using one or two touch they can earn themselves the space to drive forward and into a goal scoring position. Quick movement off the ball is very hard to stop as you cannot close or pressure the players as quickly as you would like. The player in the middle should be encouraged to play side on and to receive on his back foot before passing. After completing the passes, the player must dribble out of the area at top speed and shoot.

SET-UP

- A group of players and a keeper as shown in the diagram.
- The first player goes out as a forward while the next player acts as a midfielder.
- The start, the coach passes into the midfielder who receives the ball side on and on his back foot, then turns and looks to play a through pass avoiding the flags/defenders and into the forward's path. The forward has complete freedom on where he starts and where he runs but he must use good variation, movements and timing to not be offside.
- For the next attack the midfielder becomes the forward.

THOUGHTS

Often we run sessions where each player knows exactly where to pass and where to run. This is not game realistic. In this practice I have tried to make it as close to the real game as possible. The midfielder turns and does not know where his forward is or where he is going to run. Therefore he must get his head up and must play a good pass. The forward also has to time his run well to get away from the defenders at a realistic pace and also to not be offside.

SET-UP

⊛ Two teams of players and a keeper as shown in the diagram. Each team has two wide players. One team on the right, one team on the left. The players in the middle work in pairs.

⊛ To start, the two wide players put themselves in position of a full back and winger. The full back passes to the winger and overlaps. The wide player has two choices, he can pass down the line for the overlapping full back or use the full back as a decoy and dribble inside to attack. In the box is a 2v2 situation. For the next attack the players change roles.

⊛ Crosses alternate from the left and right side of the pitch.

THOUGHTS

This practice looks at the roles of an attacking full back and wide player when in possession and the choices and options that an overlapping run gives to the team. A pass down to the overlapping player will signal an out-swinging cross to the forwards and a cut inside will signal an in-swinging ball into the box. How do the forwards react? What changes in movement do they make?

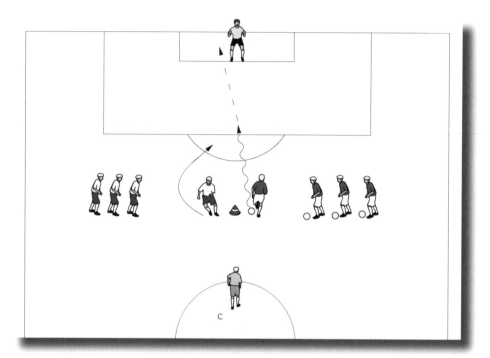

SET-UP

◉ Two groups of players and a keeper as shown in the diagram. The players work in pairs and alternate between defenders and forwards.

◉ The forwards have the ball at their feet and are facing the goal approximately 20 yards out while the defender is in line with the forward but facing away from goal. The forward starts the practice and on his first touch the duel commences.

THOUGHTS

This practice looks at the forward's decision on his first touch when given the opportunity to race clear of the defense and also at the speed and decisiveness in his play in order to make sure he takes his chance. The defender works hard on his reactions and recovery speed and should be advised that any type of pressure or recovery challenge will put the striker under more pressure to score.

SET-UP

* Two groups of players and two keepers as shown in the diagram.

* To start, the coach serves balls for the players to finish first time. This practice is a competition between the two groups as to who scores 5 goals first.

* The session can be used for various types of finishing: heading, volleying and first time shooting.

THOUGHTS

This practice gives the players a chance to work on various finishing techniques under pressure to score, due to competitive competition from the other team. The players really enjoy this edge to the game and concentrate hard on their techniques in order to score. I use this often and prefer to only use heading as this is one part of youth soccer which most player don't like. This practice helps to develop this technique in a fun way.

SET-UP

⊛ A group of players, one keeper and one coach as shown in the diagram.

⊛ The first player receives a pass then dribbles to shoot with power from outside the box. Immediately after shooting, the coach passes him another ball just inside the box. The player must now react using placement, guiding the ball past the keeper and into the net.

THOUGHTS

This practice guides a player's shooting technique in a game. The practice tells a player that outside the box, using power gives you the best chance to score but once inside the box the better choice is placement or even dribbling the keeper.

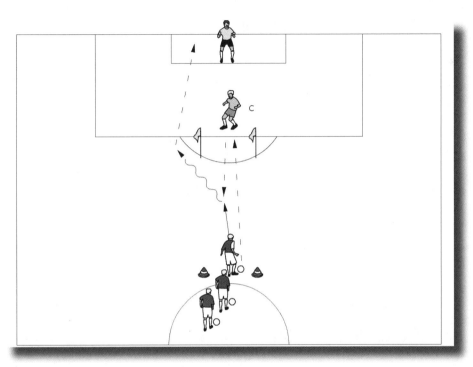

SET-UP

⊛ A group of players and a keeper as shown in the diagram. The coach acts as the server.

⊛ To start the practice the first player passes into the coach and supports to receive a varied lay off [on floor, in air or bouncing]. The player must judge this return pass and with the first touch go past the flag to the right or left and then shoot at goal with the second touch.

THOUGHTS

This practice looks at a midfielder supporting his initial pass forward and then having the ability to use his first touch into space in order to get a shot at goal. This practice simulates a real game situation as often when a ball is set back from a forward to an onrushing midfielder, the defending players run out to pressure and only the players who are aware and have a very good first touch are able to avoid these pressuring defenders and get a shot at goal.

SET-UP

⊛ A group of players, two servers and a keeper as shown in the diagram.

⊛ To start the practice, the forward pulls off the flag/pole and receives a pass from coach one. The forward takes their first touch out of their feet and across the flag and shots with their right foot. Immediately they react and then pulls off the defender to receive a second pass from coach two. This time the player controls across their body in order to finish with their left foot.

THOUGHTS

This practice looks at the forwards sharp movements and good first touch in order to give them a chance to score. The player has to work both their left and right foot in order to take these chances and this will give the coach plenty of opportunities to offer advice on which foot to receive the ball on and what technique to sue in order to beat the defender/ flag.

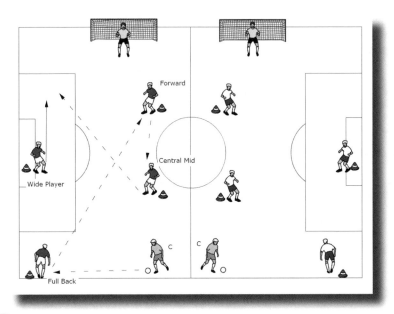

SET-UP

⊛ Two teams, one on each half of the pitch, with goalkeepers as shown in the diagram.

⊛ SAME SIDE OF PITCH

1. into full back, full back into forward, forward sets midfielder, midfielder down the line for wide player (shown).

2. full back into midfielder who moves off to receive, midfielder into forward , forward opens and plays down the line for wide player.

3. into wide player, wide player sets full back, full back into forward who sets midfielder, midfielder down the line for wide player.

4. full back into wide player, wide player dribbles inside and passes to midfielder, midfielder passes down the line for full back.

5. full back into forward, forward sets midfielder, midfielder square to onrushing full back, full back down the line for wide player to run onto.

SWITCH PLAY

1. full back into forward who sets midfielder, midfielder opens, dribbles and switches to opposite wide player. Forwards attack crosses from opposite side.

2. full back into center midfielder, center midfielder switches to opposite full back, full back dribbles and passes down the line for wide player to run onto. Forwards attack crosses from opposite side.

3. full back into forward who sets wide player, wide player inside to midfielder who switches play to other wide player. Forwards attack crosses from opposite side.

4. full back into midfielder who opens and plays to opposite forward, forward receives safe side and opens to play down the line for wide player. Forwards attack crosses from opposite side.

5. full back into forward, forward receives and passes to opposite midfielder, midfielder opens and passes out to wide player. Forward attacks cross from opposite side.

SET-UP

⊛ Two groups of players and one keeper as shown in the diagram.

⊛ To start the practice the coach throws the ball over the first flag/pole and the first receiving player must run, take a touch to the side and past the second flag/pole in order to shoot at goal.

⊛ The coach then serves the opposite line. A competition between the two lines can be added with the coach counting the number of goals before the players switch sides and work on the other foot.

THOUGHTS

Often young players are easily distracted by defenders when trying to control an aerial pass to the floor, this session gives the player lots of practice at relaxing in this situation. Also it helps to work on a good first touch into space and past defenders in order to shoot at goal. Later, as the players' confidence develops, you may wish to add a recovery defender rather than the first flag/pole.

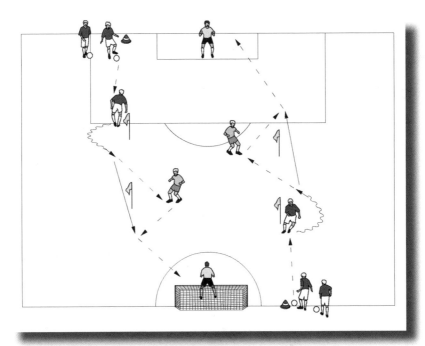

SET-UP

- ⊛ Two groups of players, two coaches and two keepers as shown in the diagram.

- ⊛ To start, the first player passes into the attacker who checks off his marker to turn and beat him with a skill and then accelerate away to play a one-two with the coach before shooting at goal.

- ⊛ This time the player stays tight to his marker and beats him with a quick turn before dribbling to play a one-two and finishing.

- ⊛ This time the player sets back to the initial passer and spins off to the right or left in order to receive a return pass before accelerating away to play a one-two and finishing.

THOUGHTS

This practice is set up to teach players the importance of changing speed after doing well to beat a tight marker. Many young players beat a player but the team doesn't get the best advantage from this good play as the player doesn't then accelerate away or make the correct decisions. The practice can be progressed and modified in many ways after the initial skill past the defender, for instance the player could then accelerate away to cross for a teammate or make a through pass.

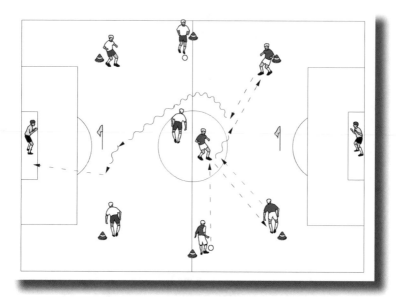

SET-UP

- Two teams of five players (including keepers) as shown in the diagram.
- To start, the first player passes into the midfielder who is under pressure. Since he can't pass forward he receives with an open body and on his left foot to pass out to his teammate diagonally behind. Then he checks to receive the ball back and opens out off his right foot to pass diagonally to his teammate. Then he checks to receive the ball for a third time but now is given the call to turn as he has space. He turns and dribbles to beat the flag/pole and get a shot at goal.

PROGRESSION

- A progression to this practice is to add a center forward in front of the flag who, as the midfielder gets the call to turn, spins off the flag and receives a through pass from the midfielder to score.
- Players move to the next station to their right after each attack, and after shooting they join the back of their line.

> **THOUGHTS**
>
> This session is for midfielders who must learn to be patient in their build up and look to move the ball quickly to teammates and show good movements in order to lose tight markers, make the space to turn and accelerate away to attack. The progression works excellently as the midfielder must turn, accelerate then get his head up to see his teammate's run and then find him with an accurate pass. This practice covers many aspects of a midfielder's game.

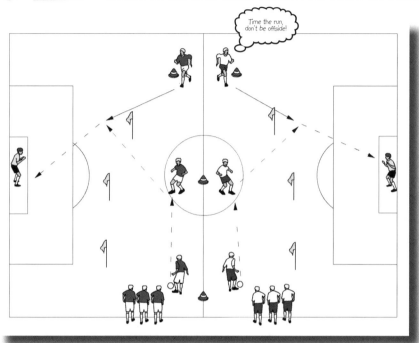

SET-UP

⊛ Two groups of players, two keepers and six flags/poles as shown in the diagram.

⊛ The first player passes inside to the center midfielder who has checked away and back to receive on his back foot. The midfielder turns and dribbles across the pitch to play a diagonal pass in-between the center flag/pole and the furthest flag/pole. The wide attacker must time his run to not be offside and run at the correct speed and angle in order to get a goal scoring opportunity.

⊛ All players move up a place on the pitch for the next attack.

THOUGHTS

This session looks at when a team opens out and tries to switch play. Often the opposition's defenders sit back and allow the ball to be played out to your wide player, but there are occasions when the defender gets too tight or caught in a bad position. Now we can use the space in behind the defender. The wide player must use good timing, speed and the correct angle to ensure that he gets away from the defender and has a chance to score.

SET-UP

- ⊛ A group of players and a keeper as shown in the diagram.

- ⊛ The session has three stations A,B, and C. Player A works as a rebounder, player B is the defender, player C is the shooter. After each attack the players move up a position with the shooter going to the end of the line and waiting another turn.

- ⊛ The coach passes into the shooter who must receive with an open body position and finish quickly across the keeper. As soon as the coach passes to the shooter, the defender tries to get across to the keeper, defender or post.

THOUGHTS

This very short, sharp practice has lots of good habits for the players to learn. First the shooter is pressured to get a shot in at goal very quickly and then he must remember to shoot across goal giving him more opportunity to score. The defender must react quickly and never stand to see the outcome of the shot but try everything to get across and put the striker off by forcing him wide or making a challenge. The rebounding player must also stay alert, as many goals are scored with simple tap-in rebounds.

SET-UP

⊛ One keeper, two teams of four players. Each team has two wide players and two attackers/defenders in the box as shown in the diagram.

⊛ The coach passes out and down the line to one of the wide players. The wide player crosses to his teammates acting as the attackers in a 2v2 situation. As soon as the ball leaves play the coach then passes out wide to the opposite team who now cross for their teammates who have changed roles from defenders to attackers. The game continues until a certain time elapses, a number of goals are scored or a number of crosses are made.

THOUGHTS

This game looks at the ability of the wide players to cross accurately to their teammates and at the forwards' movements to lose defenders in and around the penalty box. The role reversal part of the game is crucial as this is when the movements to lose players is made and when a coach can see which players switch off or don't react at the speed required. The practice is hard work for the group but the players enjoy the quickness, the number of goals and the competitive edge between the two teams.

SET-UP

- Two groups of four players and a keeper as shown in the diagram. Each team numbers their players 1 to 4 with number 1 going into the box while 2,3 and 4 spreading around the outside with a ball at their feet.

- The coach starts by calling out a color. The player in the middle of that team attacks first and must lose the defender, receive a pass from one of his teammates and try to score. If a goal is scored or the ball leaves play the roles immediately reverse and now the defending player becomes an attacker and looks to receive a pass from one of his teammates in order to score.

- The players continue until all six balls are played. Then number 2's play against each other.

THOUGHTS
This game looks at quick movements to lose defenders and receive a pass, the ability to use disguise, skill and strength in order to get a shot at goal, and the ability to defend with patience and react to the next ball. This game is both fun and competitive and this comes across in practice as the teams and players work to beat each other.

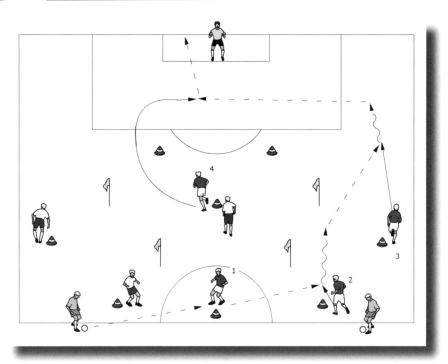

SET-UP

- Two coaches work as servers with the players spread out across the stations as shown in the diagram.
- to start the first coach passes into the center midfielder at station 1, the midfielder opens out and switches play to his full back at station 2, the full back dribbles forward to attack the flag/defender, the wide player at station 3 makes a run outside and down the flank. The full back passes in the wide player's path and the wide player crosses into the box for the forward at station 4 to shoot at goal.
- Each player moves up to the next station on the pitch. The next attack starts with the 2nd coach and builds up down the opposite flank.

THOUGHTS

This session looks at the team building up with a quick switch of play and the use of attacking; forward thinking full backs that want to get advanced quickly. The tempo and type of pass is a specific area of importance and also the pace of the player's movements and dribbling. I encourage the young players to cross low and hard to the forwards, whilst the forwards must make a run away from the area in which they wish to receive the cross.

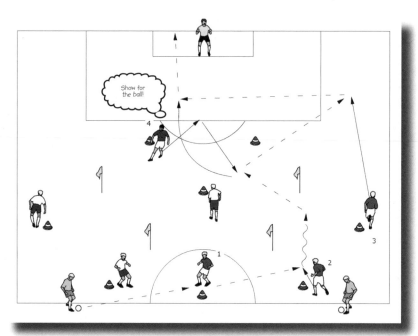

SET-UP

⊚ Same as in previous session

⊚ To start, the coach passes into the center midfielder at station 1 who opens and switches play to his full back at station 2. The full back now decides to pass directly into his forward at station 4 who has made a run in behind before checking back in front of the flag/defender to receive. The forward then plays the ball down the line for the supporting wide player at station 3 and then makes a run into the box to receive the cross.

⊚ The players all move up a station and the next attack starts with the 2nd coach and builds up down the opposite side of the pitch.

THOUGHTS

This session progresses nicely from the previous one and still sees the quick switch of play in attack and the advancing full back getting forward at pace. This time he chooses to pass into his forward who has made a clever run to lose his marker and now he releases the wide player before spinning into the area to receive the cross. The two sessions give the full back valuable passing options and therefore knowledge in possession of the ball. Also it gives the wide player another option should he be stuck with a tight marker.

Conclusion

I hope the sessions in this book and the topics raised will aid you in your careers as soccer coaches. The roles we have to cover as a coach are vast and include being a teacher, manager of people, friend and role model to our players.

My personal view is that too many coaches judge themselves solely on team results and whether players go on to senior youth and first team soccer. This is very unrealistic for the majority and the questions I would rather see answered are:

Do my players improve?
Do they enjoy soccer?
Are they nice people?

If I can answer with a yes to the above questions then I feel that my job as a youth coach is complete. There are very few that make it to the top level of the game whether it's because they don't possess the necessary natural ability, physical characteristics or enough support. Therefore we should dedicate ourselves to giving every child who attends our sessions the best possible experience that enables them to improve, develop as people and enjoy the game. Remember, often the ones that don't make the top level as players will stay in the game as managers, coaches and referees.

Once again I hope this book has been of some help. Please feel free to e-mail me any questions or feedback to my personal address:

mbeale4980@aol.com

10/08

154